THE PEACEMAKERS OF
NIEMBA

The full story of the Congo ambush

TOM McCAUGHREN

SOMERVILLE PRESS

ROINN AN TAOISIGH

BAILE ATHA CLIATH 2

The story of the men of our Defence Forces
who died at Niemba, in the service of the
United Nations in the cause of world peace,
is, truly, in the highest traditions of Irish
military history.

In the pages which follow Tom McCaughren
tells this moving story with understanding and
with sympathy. Wisely he lets the facts
speak for themselves. There is no attempt
to exaggerate — no attempt to over-dramatize.
But drama there is in almost every page. The
trials and tribulations of such an expedition,
the joy and the sadness, the laughter and the
tears, the triumphs and the failures — they are
all here in the story which Tom McCaughren
has to tell. The research which he has
undertaken brings to light much new material
and several hitherto unpublished facts.

The story of Niemba is, indeed, well
worth the telling. It tells of brave men, of
gallant deeds and of tragic events. The
dedicated and inspiring devotion to duty
shown by those who died at Niemba — as well as
those who survived — must surely merit a well
informed documentary record such as Tom
McCaughren has now provided and which he has
so aptly entitled "The Peacemakers of
Niemba".

The author and all who co-operated with
him in his work deserve our appreciation and
our thanks.

SEAN LEMASS

*To the Irish soldiers who died at Niemba and
elsewhere in the Congo in the cause of world peace*

On November 8th, 1960, a United Nations patrol of 11 Irish soldiers was ambushed by Baluba warriors in Katanga Province of the Congo. Forced in self-defence to do the last thing they wanted to do—open fire—they inflicted many casualties on their attackers before nine of them—including the patrol leader Lt. Kevin Gleeson—were finally overwhelmed. These nine soldiers were the first members of the Irish Army to die in action abroad and in the cause of world peace and their deaths were the first big loss of the U.N. peace force in the Congo.

In 1964 the Irish Government, in conjunction with the United Nations Secretariat, gave the author access to the official files on the ambush. Two years of research followed. As well as examining the files, he conducted exhaustive interviews with many of the military personnel involved together with numerous follow-up inquiries at home and abroad. He also obtained more previously unpublished material in the form of personal letters, diaries and photographs from relatives and comrades of the men on that ill-fated patrol. The result was the first documentary account, not only of the ambush, but of the dramatic events which led to and followed it. The ranks given are those held at the time.

Somerville Press,
Dromore, Bantry,
Co. Cork, Ireland

First published by Browne & Nolan Ltd 1966
This new edition by Somerville Press 2013

Designed by Jane Stark
seamistgraphics@gmail.com
Typeset in Adobe Garamond

ISBN: 978 0 9573461 1 6

Printed and bound in Spain by
GraphyCems, Villatuerta, Navarra

CONTENTS

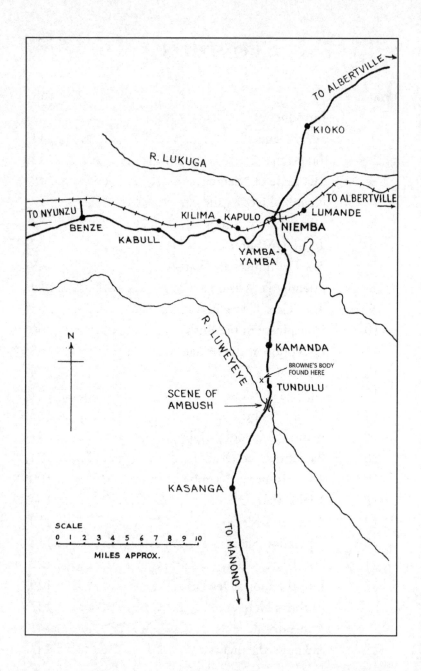

TO ALBERTVILLE

KIOKO

R. LUKUGA

TO NYUNZU   TO ALBERTVILLE

KILIMA   KAPULO   LUMANDE
BENZE   NIEMBA
        KABULL
                        YAMBA-
                        YAMBA

R. LUWEYEYE

N

                        KAMANDA

                        BROWNE'S BODY
                        FOUND HERE
                        x
SCENE OF   TUNDULU
AMBUSH

KASANGA

SCALE
0 1 2 3 4 5 6 7 8 9 10
MILES APPROX.

TO MANONO

6

Introduction

It's now more than fifty years since the first United Nations peacekeeping mission in the Congo, and peacekeepers are back there. The main trouble this time is in the north-eastern provinces of Kivu and Orientale, rather than Katanga, but the problems seem eerily familiar—outside support for rebels, serious abuses and violations of human rights, acts of violence against civilians . . . attacks on peacekeepers and humanitarian personnel . . . illegal exploitation of natural resources... These are not my words but of the Security Council, and those who took part in the first U.N. mission may be forgiven for asking, what has changed? What was it all for, the blood, the sweat and the tears?

Today the peacekeepers are members of the United Nations Organisation Stabilisation Mission. In 1960 they were known simply as the United Nations Organisation in the Congo. For many of those who went there from Ireland it was their first time to go abroad, let alone to Africa. They found themselves in a country the size of Western Europe, one of the richest in the world in terms of mineral wealth, yet one of the poorest. Its mineral wealth had been exploited before, and it had just got its independence from Belgium. However, it quickly descended into chaos and Belgian troops returned to protect their nationals. At the same time, Belgian mining interests were slow to let go of their former colony and encouraged the particularly wealthy province of Katanga to secede.

Compared with Lebanon, where for over twenty years successive Irish battalions of about 600 troops each kept the peace in an area of 52 square miles (136 square kilometres), the Congo was a vast area in which to operate. Ireland had two battalions in the Congo and they were very thinly spread. To give some idea of just how thin on the ground they were, Col. Harry Byrne, commander of the Eastern Provinces, noted shortly after the Niemba ambush that the U.N. had a total of 1,500 troops deployed over an area of north Katanga as large as England and Wales.

However, the U.N. soldiers succeeded in preserving the new republic's independence and stabilising a fragile international situation. Tiny as Ireland is in comparison with the Congo, it played an important part in that achievement. It was the first time that members of its Defence Forces were on such a mission and it was the beginning of a great learning curve for them and for those who sent them. As a result, Irish troops are recognised today as being among the best peacekeepers in the world, and at the time of writing there are 440 Defence Forces personnel serving in 17 missions across 15 different countries.

The Congo lesson, however, was an expensive one in terms of human life. The Irish soldiers were ill-prepared and ill-equipped and within a short time nine of them were killed by tribesmen. The incident, on November 8th 1960, occurred near the village of Niemba in northern Katanga. People knew very little about the incident at the time, apart from the fact that the patrol had been ambushed by Baluba warriors; that in the ensuing battle eight of the soldiers had been killed, two had survived and one was missing.

Four years later I decided to find out more about had happened and in 1966 published the results in this book. I thought that people then—and now— would want to know why the ambush had occurred and how well-armed soldiers could have been killed by tribesmen armed with bows and arrows. I wanted to get access to documents, including letters and notes recorded by army personnel and relatives at a time when these were still available. I also wanted to interview as many military personnel as I could who were directly involved as well as relatives of the dead soldiers when memories were still fresh as time can distort the memory.

I was asked on a couple of occasions by army people why I didn't call my book, the Peace*keepers* rather than the Peace*makers* of Niemba. The answer is simple. The platoon of about 40 soldiers was sent to Niemba from its headquarters in Albertville. This was a distance of 86 miles (138 kilometres) by road—almost as far as from Dublin to Belfast. It was 20 miles (32 kilometres) shorter by train, but the service was often disrupted by the activities of Baluba warriors. By either route, it was a long way from base.

Bloody clashes had taken place between the gendarmerie—Katangan soldiers operating with Belgian officers—and the Baluba of north Katanga who were opposed to the new secessionist regime. The inhabitants of Niemba had suffered at the hands of both, and the platoon was stationed there with the object, among other things, of giving them protection.

However, unlike modern day peacekeepers who are equipped with armoured troop carriers and high tech radio communications, the small Niemba garrison had only the use of two vehicles, a Landrover and a Volkswagen pickup, neither of which offered protection or had radio communications. They were in a very hostile situation and could not *keep* the peace, but they did their best to *make* peace and help people in any way they could, often at the peril of their lives, as for example, when they rescued a priest called Fr. Peeters.

The problem that led to the ambush is clear now but, perhaps, was not so clear then. The U.N. had brokered an agreement to prevent clashes between the gendarmerie and the Baluba. As part of that agreement the U.N. force was to keep the roads open. However, the Baluba in the Niemba area continued to block the roads by felling trees and destroying bridges, presumably to consolidate their position and keep the gendarmerie out. When the troops in Niemba attempted to reopen one of the roads, they were ambushed by Baluba warriors and nine of them died.

When I asked to see the Army files on the ambush in 1964, my request was refused. At that time I was a reporter and Defence Correspondent in *The Irish Times* in Dublin. The Political Correspondent was Michael McInerney and I was aware that he and other political correspondents got a weekly briefing from the Taoiseach, Sean Lemass. I wrote a letter to the Taoiseach asking him for permission to view the files and interview military personnel. Michael gave it to the Taoiseach who replied that he would contact the Minister for Defence, Gerald Bartley. As a result I got a letter from the Minister giving me permission. I was subsequently told that, out of consideration for the relatives, details of the injuries sustained by the soldiers would not be available for publication.

I was conscious of the fact that I was doing my research a relatively short time after the ambush and when I spoke to some of the families I could see that they were still very traumatised by what had happened. They were very helpful in providing letters and other information about their loved ones and the proviso apart, I had no wish to add to their suffering by dwelling on medical matters. That being said, they would read the graphic account of one of the survivors, Private Thomas Kenny, who described the injuries inflicted on him.

My priority was to find out as much as I could about how the ambush had occurred and the circumstances surrounding it, and I told my publisher, Jeremy Addis of Browne & Nolan, that I believed I had unearthed 98% of the information available.

My research took two years to do and I found that there were conflicting emotions and concerns about various aspects of the ambush, including the fact that one member of the patrol, Trooper Anthony Browne had not been found in the original search. Questions raised subsequently about how long

Browne may have survived the battle and the part played by him in the survival of Private Kenny are dealt with in the Author's Note.

Some officers had concerns about other matters. One, for example, was worried about details of Operation Shamrock being made public. During the operation, which required considerable courage, troops removed a number of wounded warriors from their hospital beds in a Baluba town in the middle of the night. Several of them were later handed over to their enemies, the Katangan authorities, for trial. The officer was concerned that the ethics of this operation might be questioned. However his concerns were allayed when Sean Lemass agreed to write a foreword to the book, thus, by implication, endorsing the actions that had been taken.

Until I did my research, the public were not aware that some of the warriors had been brought to court for their part in the ambush. According to the judgment, which is given in the book, the aspirant fighters were sprinkled with "magic water" which, they were told would shield them from gunfire. However, there was nothing in the judgment, or in the reports I read, to show that the warriors engaged in any acts of cannibalism after the ambush, contrary to speculation at the time. The "magic water" may have protected some of them, but one report a week after the ambush indicated that 25 Baluba were killed and another 25 were missing.

In addition to personal weapons, Lt. Gleeson's patrol had two rapid-firing light machine guns called Bren guns. Had they deployed these and had they been able to use them (the warriors were almost on top of them when they unleased their first arrows) they would probably have won the battle. But at what cost? A hundred Baluba dead? Two hundred? How would that have looked back home? I suggest it would have been seen as a massacre by Irish peacekeepers.

I remember the first troops being told before they left Dublin that they carried the honour of their country with them and not to let it down. The last thing they wanted to do was open fire on those they had come to help. Lt. Gleeson appears to have taken the view that he and his men could only survive in such a hostile environment by assisting the local people and using friendly persuasion on those who were not so friendly. It took a lot of courage to do so, and nine of them paid for it with their lives.

TOM McCAUGHREN, 2013

ONE

Sorry General!

The young lieutenant wiped the sweat from his brow with his hand and pushed back his blue helmet. Anxiously his eyes followed the aircraft circling the huge jungle air base. Then he switched his gaze to the long rows of Belgian paratroops—500 in all—drawn up on parade on the tarmac 300 yards away. The Belgian officer had warned him of the consequences if one Belgian were killed. But the plane now about to land had failed to identify itself, and the young lieutenant had his orders. He had to arrest the plane and detain its occupants if necessary.

The plane came in low over the bush, touched down and taxied up the runway. The lieutenant had put a row of soldiers across its path, and now he loaded his Gustaf sub-machine gun. Another officer was behind him in the jeep. All weapons were at the ready. The plane stopped, and four or five top-ranking Belgian officers got out. The young lieutenant explained the position. Then one of the arrivals was introduced—General Gheysen, supreme commander of the Belgian forces in the Congo. Lt. Kevin Gleeson of the 33rd Irish Battalion of the United Nations Peace Force grinned and apologised.

The date was August 30th 1960. Chaos had broken out in the newly-independent Republic of the Congo. Administrative and public services had broken down. There had been mutinies in the National Army with consequent outbursts of violence against Europeans, and Belgium had flown in troops to protect her nationals. In response to a request from the Congolese Government, the Security Council had passed a resolution calling on Belgium to withdraw her troops and authorising the U.N. Secretary General, Mr Hammarskjold to provide the Government with the military assistance necessary until the national security forces could "meet fully their tasks".

However, while Belgium had begun the evacuation of her troops, elements of the United Nations Peace Force had entered Katanga Province in the face of threatened resistance by Mr. Tshombé, President of the Provincial Government, which had proclaimed the independence of the province.

Ireland's initial contribution to the U.N. Peace Force towards the end of July 1960 was one battalion, the 32nd, which was deployed in Kivu Province to the north of Katanga, and in the third week in August, in response to a further request from the U.N. Secretary General, she contributed another, the 33rd Battalion which was flown into Kamina, a huge former N.A.T.O. and Belgian air base in Katanga. Within a few days, however, the 33rd, with the exception of "A" Company, was transferred 500 miles north-east to riot-torn Albertville on the shore of Lake Tanganyika, to take over from a battalion of the collapsing Mali Federation of Sudan and Senegal.

"A" Company of the 33rd was left behind to take over the base from the departing Belgians and formally took command of it at midnight on August 29th. Guarding such a gigantic base was, in itself, a mammoth task for a company of 180 men, and now they assumed the additional responsibility of controlling air traffic. To add to their troubles, Central Government troops had invaded Kasai Province north-west of Katanga to put down another secessionist movement there, while others were *en route* to attempt an invasion of Katanga. This, together with the fact that the Belgians were leaving, raised the danger that an attempt would be made to seize the base.

On the 29th Mr Tshombé had arrived at the base, and 30-year-old Lt. Gleeson had turned out with a contingent to make sure that his gendarmerie did not follow. "He had seized three aircraft," Gleeson wrote on the 30th to his wife Imelda, "and it was expected that he would take control of the base. We missed him as he was going away. We had to stay in the airport until 12 o'clock today. At 10 o'clock I received word from the control tower that an unidentified plane was going to land. My instructions were to prevent the people from leaving it."

Not knowing what to expect, and not at all sure what his men could do, since the cardinal rule was they should fire only in self-defence, Gleeson's anxiety at the approach of the unidentified plane was very understandable.

He wrote to his wife: "Being in charge, I ordered my men not to fire under any circumstances, as the Belgian officer in charge warned me that if one Belgian were killed he would wipe us all out. Nevertheless, I had a job to do and I was determined to do it . . ."

Reporting the matter to his company commander, Commandant Louis Hogan, who was then also base commander, Gleeson was half afraid that in "arresting" General Gheysen, who was on a farewell tour, he did something which might become one of those embarrassing "international incidents" one was always reading about in the newspapers. However Comdt. Hogan merely laughed at the idea of a lieutenant arresting a general and said it was the best thing that could have happened. It proved to him that the Belgians manning the control tower were genuinely co-operating and as the word would soon get around, it would show all concerned that the Irish were standing for no nonsense.

To Lt. Gleeson the Gheysen affair also proved something. It was the first real test of his troops in the short time that they had come under his command. Most of them were as yet untried in battle, but from the manner in which they conducted themselves in those tense moments on the tarmac, he knew they were a good platoon.

TWO

Take Ten

From the doorway of his billet, 34-year-old Corporal Liam Dougan looked out across the vast expanse of the base, shimmering in the almost unbearable heat of the tropical sun. The Congo, he thought, was a long way from Dublin. But he had been farther. It was good few years now since he had followed his three brothers down to Dublin from Portstewart Co. Derry, to join them in the Irish Army during the emergency period of the Second World War. Then he had enlisted in the British Army, became a wireless operator, and after serving with the Royal Ulster Rifles in Hong Kong, had seen action in the jungles and rubber plantations of Malaya with the Royal Inniskilling Fusiliers. He had a near call there once when his hut was riddled with bullets, but fortunately, with the other members of his section he had been sleeping on the floor, and the only bullet to find a mark was the one that smashed the wireless set.

After a period in civvy street he had rejoined the Irish Army, become a mortar man, served on the border during the later 1950's when troops were called out to assist the civilian authorities in suppressing I.R.A. activities, and, just before he left for the Congo, passed his examination for sergeant. Like most of his fellow-soldiers he had volunteered for United Nations service not only to help the Congolese, but for such adventure as a mission of that nature might be expected to provide. So far, however, it was providing more hard work than adventure, even though reinforcements had been flown into Kamina to help them.

"We are getting very heavy duties here now since the Belgians pulled out," he wrote to his widowed mother at Cuala Road, Cabra, in Dublin adding in case she might get worried: "But we get rested just the same . . . We are having a quiet time so far, and I think the trouble is over." He went on: "We are supposed to be getting a rise, but it will be in francs. The beer out here would kill an elephant and I don't care for it, so maybe it is just as

14

well . . . We get coffee all the time and it is so nice that the lads have voted for it instead of tea."

This last remark of Dougan's however, was not 100 % correct. Twenty-one year old Private Michael McGuinn scratched his red head with the back of his biro and penned a complaint to his mother at McKee Park, North Circular Road, Dublin. He hated coffee and he asked her to send him a few packets of tea. Apart from that he was enjoying his first trip abroad. Soldiering had much more exciting possibilities than serving his time in the grocery trade in his native village of Baltinglass, Co. Wicklow. He had been in the 2nd Field Engineers, Clancy Barracks, Dublin, with his father who had been a soldier for 30 years, when the call came for volunteers for U.N. service. Both had volunteered together, but only one had been chosen. He would have liked to soldier in the Congo with his father, but virtually every member of the Army had offered their services to the U.N. and someone had to stay behind.

Having also taken a well-earned rest after a hard spell of duty, Platoon Sergeant Hugh Gaynor and some other soldiers enjoying a moment's relaxation, were making friends with a frisky little inhabitant of the bush with whom they had just made an acquaintance. This was a playful monkey, and there was great laughter as the sergeant tried to get it to sit still on his head while a photograph was taken. He smiled and thought to himself how his children would laugh if they could see him now. Later, in a letter to his wife, Betty, he joked: "If I get a copy of the photo I will send you one and you can try and figure out who is who!"

For 29-year-old Sgt. Gaynor, Congo service was a far cry from the days when he had been a motorcycle telegram boy in Dublin for the Department of Posts and Telegraphs. It was his love of motorcycles that had taken him into the 2nd Motor Squadron, there to become a regular member of the Presidential Escort. In the yard behind his little stone cottage overlooking the village of Leixlip, he had built a motorcycle with his own hands. It worked too, though admittedly it did break down a few times leaving him late for duty at Cathal Brugha Barracks in Dublin. Inevitably he would get a telling-off, but he was not one to let a thing like that worry him.

The weekend before leaving for the Congo he had managed to get away for the christening of his second son, Maurice, in the local church in Leixlip. Then, a short time before the plane was due to leave Baldonnel aerodrome, he borrowed a motorcycle and dashed out to his father-in-law's house in Chapelizod to say goodbye to the baby whom he knew would not be at the aerodrome to see him off. Members of the family who themselves were about to leave for the aerodrome were surprised when he pulled up outside the window, and as for the little lad—he was fast asleep in his moses basket.

Once more he arrived late at Cathal Brugha Barracks: the battalion had already left for the aerodrome. However, a pal had come to his rescue with a jeep, and as he told his wife later: "I never was so scared in my life, as the jeep took lumps out of the road it was going so fast."

One soldier who had good reason not to be late was 18-year-old, Trooper Thomas Fennell. From picking fruit in Raheny in Dublin he had joined the 2nd Motor Squadron to learn driving and had progressed to become a member of the Presidential Escort. He was a good boxer, having fought for St. Vincent's Club, Marino, and there was plenty of scope in the Army for that too. He was thrilled when he was selected for the 32nd Battalion and had gone to spend some leave with his grandmother in Letterkenny, Co. Donegal before the battalion mustered at the Curragh Camp, Co. Kildare. His grandmother had had six daughters and no boys, and being the eldest of a large family he was her favourite grandson. However, he had stayed a day too long in Donegal, most probably, his parents thought, because of a girl, although he never said. Due home at Clanronald Road, Donnycarney, Dublin on Friday night to be back in Cathal Brugha Barracks in time to move to the Curragh, he had not returned until the Saturday. As a result his name was taken off the battalion list. Bitterly disappointed, he volunteered for the 33rd, and considered himself lucky to have got a second opportunity.

Trooper Anthony Browne spread five cards from a newly-acquired Belgian-made pack to reveal another full house and raked in a handful of Congolese francs from under the slightly bewildered gaze of the other players. If there was one thing he was good at, it was playing cards, and what better way for a soldier to spend a few hours rest.

Born in Francis Street, Dublin, in 1941, two nights after the accidental German bombing of houses in the North Strand area, he was, in his father's words, "so small you wouldn't have given tuppence of copper for him." However, he had grown up into a self-reliant man, small but hardy. He learned to play cards in Fatima Mansions, a block of Corporation flats in Rialto to which the family had moved, and he seldom lost. He tried a few jobs, including messenger, before joining the Army and ending up in the 2nd Motor Squadron.

Browne never did make the Presidential Escort, but he was quite happy. The Army provided a regular job, a wage that enabled him to contribute to his home and keep himself in the rather "loud" clothes for which he had a great liking. He had made up his mind to leave, however, when he was not selected for the 32nd Battalion. Then he found himself on the 33rd and was absolutely delighted. His only regret was that he had to leave at a time when his mother was in St. Kevin's Hospital for an operation, but he managed to get away from the Curragh to visit her the weekend before he left. Originally he was with company headquarters, but he was not happy there and put in for a transfer. His request was granted and now he was with Lt. Gleeson's platoon.

Someone said: "Okay Willie, it's your turn to deal", and when there was no reaction someone else quipped: "Poor Davis, doesn't even know his own name." Private Davis laughed and said: "Count me out boys." Lying in his bunk, he reflected that he should have been used to the name Willie by now. He smiled to himself when he thought back on how it had happened. He had worked in Dublin first as a messenger, then as a storeman, and did not like either job. What he wanted was to join the Army. But he had to be 17 and he was not then 16. He would never forget the look on the recruiting officer's face when he took in his baptismal certificate, suitably altered.

"Were you ever in jail?" the officer asked. "No," he replied, his face getting very red. "Well you will be," said the officer, "if you don't get that piece of paper and yourself out of here."

The next thing his mother knew, however, he had succeeded in enlisting. "Do you know Paddy is after joining the Army?" his mother, Mrs. Catherine Davis asked one of his pals. "Paddy is right," laughed the pal. "He isn't Paddy any more, he's Willie!" Then she understood why he had asked her about his brother Willie who had been born before him, but who had died at the age of three months. It had been a simple matter for him to get a copy of Willie's baptismal certificate from the pro-Cathedral, Marlborough Street, Dublin, and being a fine lad for his age, no one suspected he was not who the certificate said he was—Willie Davis. Of course, he had presented himself to a different officer the second time, just in case. When, two years later, he was selected for Congo service, his mother had half threatened to expose him, but he knew she would not. She was too fond of him to spoil his chance of foreign service. So she kept his secret, and so did his brother Seamus who was in West Berlin with the Royal Engineers. They addressed their letters to "Private W. Davis", but inside they wrote, "Dear Paddy . . ." Apart from his best friend Private Peter Donnelly, few others knew his secret. There was, therefore, little danger of it getting out. Unless, of course, he was killed, and then it would not matter. Anyway, he thought, this was a peace mission, and no one was going to get killed on a peace mission.

Twenty-five-year-old Corporal Peter Kelly shouted across at "Dougie", his friend Corporal Dougan, and asked him for the time. Before leaving Dublin, Kelly had taken off the watch which his wife had given him as a birthday present, and pressing it into her hand had told her: "You keep that Lil." She had protested, of course, but he had insisted. "Go on, you keep it," he had told her. He wanted her to have something to remember him by—in case anything went wrong.

Unknown to any of these men, time for them and for some of their comrades was running out. In only a few weeks, 20-year-old Private Joseph Fitzpatrick, who was sitting nearby sketching, would have the grim task of sketching for a search party the location of the bodies of several of his friends in an bloody battlefield near Niemba. Already the train of events that was to draw these men to that fateful spot was in motion.

THREE

The Rape of Niemba

While the United Nations force used its good offices to bring about a ceasefire agreement in the Kasai-Katanga border areas, it also had to contend with the conflict between the Baluba of North Katanga who favoured Mr. Lamumba, the Congo Premier, and Tshombé's Belgian-officered gendarmerie.

Referring to the conflict in a report to the U.N. Secretary-General, Mr Hammarskjold's Special Representative in the Congo, Mr. Rajeshwar Dayal, stated that "the presence in central and northern Katanga of heavily-armed gendarmerie units under the command of Belgian officers" had been for some time "a source of irritation to the Baluba tribes opposed to the present Katangan authorities." The prevailing state of tension, he reported, increased to the point where, on September 13th and 14th, groups of armed Baluba engaged the forces at Manono, a tin-mining town about half-way between Kamina and Albertville.

The 33rd Battalion's "B" Company, under Commandant Pearse Barry, was then stationed in Manono, it being one of a number of points in an area the size of Ireland which the battalion had been ordered to occupy. Before the revolt, a tense situation had existed between the Baluba, who represented about 95% of the population, and the local administration which was still Belgian in character.

Two minor clashes occurred on the 13th, and on the morning of the 14th the Baluba attacked the Territoire Building, which was defended by Belgian administrative officials and Belgian officered Katangan police. In accordance with a pre-arranged plan Comdt. Barry gave refuge to European mining personnel, nuns and traders, and to the wives and children of the police. Later the officials and the police laid down their arms and also were given protection. Having secured the airstrip, Comdt. Barry was then able to evacuate all those who wished to leave. In the battle 25 Baluba had been killed and as

19

many wounded, while the only casualties on the other side were two policemen wounded. The situation had been helped somewhat by the fact that a gendarmerie unit camped in the town had not participated in the action. But the Irish camp was now in danger of attack. The company, however, succeeded in calming the Baluba, then opened the roads and evacuated 15 injured to hospital where they were treated by the company doctor, Comdt. Arthur Beckett.

An Officer Board appointed by the Irish Army Chief of Staff which later was to recommend the posthumous award of the Military Medal for Gallantry to Trooper Browne, also recommended Comdt. Barry for promotion to the rank of lieutenant colonel in recognition of "courage and leadership of a high order" in saving the lives of 250 people on this occasion.

While peace was thus restored in Manono, trouble erupted in other areas. "On the following day," Mr. Dayal reported, "the United Nations forces averted a clash between the Balubakat (members of Baluba movement opposed to secession of Katanga) and the pro-Tshombé Conakat workers at the nearby coal-mine of Luena, but were unable to persuade the demonstrators to disperse. On the afternoon of that day, however, and when the situation appeared to be relatively stable, a train with two seemingly empty carriages arrived at the station of Luena; there emerged a force of 95 Katangese gendarmes, including 30 special recruits, who immediately took up positions. On the other side of a wire barrier there was a large crowd of Baluba, many of them armed with primitive weapons or bicycle chains. After a short interval, the gendarmerie opened fire on the crowd, and after dispersing it, despatched patrols in various directions which hunted down and shot numerous Baluba, some of whom had offered no resistance to the patrol's advance."

"On 16th September," continued Mr. Dayal, "further patrols were sent by the gendarmerie into neighbouring villages, which were subsequently found by United Nations troops to be deserted, with several dwellings burnt. Two truckloads of prisoners were taken out of Luena by the gendarmerie. The trucks were later found abandoned by the roadside, and the United Nations troops counted 68 dead, all of them Baluba. There were no casualties on the side of the gendarmerie."

"As was to be expected," said Mr. Dayal, "this brutal repressive operation and raids which were carried out by the Katangese gendarmerie in the towns of Niemba, Kabalo (both directly west of Albertville) and Mitwaba (south of Manono) aroused the feelings of the local population to a degree bordering on desperation. In some cases, as in Luena, the civilian population sought the protection of the United Nations forces, but in general, the desire was to take revenge, whatever the risks involved."

It was the occurrence at Niemba that was to bring Lt. Gleeson and his platoon there from Kamina. It happened early in October.

Although one company short, and with many of his remaining men constantly occupied guarding widely-scattered towns and installations, Lt. Col. Richard Bunworth, commander of the 33rd Battalion, was extending his patrols in a programme designed to show the United Nations flag and help pacify the huge area under his command. The first long-range patrol, under Comdt. Patrick Keogh, set out from battalion headquarters in the Regina Pacis Convent, Albertville on September 26th to drive west along the 86-mile twisting red dust road to Niemba and south some 116 miles on the equally dusty Manono road as far as Kiambi ferry. The 70 men of this patrol were the first Irish troops to visit Niemba and were welcomed in the village, which they found to be a small trading station built on a road junction, near the Albertville-Kamina railway line, and surrounded by many Baluba villages.

Overlooking as it did the River Lukuga, they thought it was a rather nice place. The troops purchased petrol from a villa and goods from a shop, both staffed by local inhabitants. They also bought bunches of bananas from other villagers. They were told that the natives would be friendly down as far as the Esa River. On the journey south the troops noticed smoke from large fires out in the bush and natives whom they met told them, through their Swedish interpreter, Lt. Stig von Beyer, that the fires had been started by pygmies.

The bridge at Kinsukulu, about 35 miles below Niemba, was down, and as the engineer officer, Lt. Walter Raftery, and a party set about repairing it, a band of Baluba wearing skin caps marched out of the village on the far side in military fashion, chanting and waving a variety of weapons, including spears, bows and arrows, bicycle chains and "bundooki" (a crude home made gun), as they approached. Comdt. Keogh deployed his men in defensive positions at the bridge, and with his second-in-command, Captain "Big Jim" Flynn, the interpreter and several soldiers went forward to meet them. By this time other Baluba were closing in through the bush. Then, when the marchers were about 20 yards away they halted, again in a military fashion which was impressive, in a savage sort of way. Keogh and his men cocked their sub-machine guns in expectation of an attack, but when the Baluba heard that the strangers were "Onee" as they called O.N.U. (Organisation des Nations Unies) they welcomed them.

Although under the influence of "bangi-bangi", a local hemp drug, the tribesmen became quite friendly, warned them that the Baluba farther on were very hostile and provided them with a guide, a young spear-carrying warrior wearing headskin, shirt and ragged trousers.

Sitting on the bonnet of Keogh's jeep, this guide led the patrol south, across the Esa River, past several burned-out villages, and through numerous roadblocks, each consisting of a light branch and a few European-type chairs. The natives manning the roadblocks ran into the bush, except at one where the guide took fright and fled and a rather aggressive warrior armed with a "bundooki" jumped on and took the patrol into Senge Tshimbo, a village about 44 miles short of Kiambi. There the patrol spent the night in a stone building which Belgians had built as a European lodging house. It was a rather cheerless place, being completely devoid of furniture or any other simple comforts, and Comdt. Malachy McMahon, acting intelligence officer of the battalion, was later to recall how one of the soldiers sleeping on the ground, rested his head on his handkerchief—his only contact with civilisation. However, that soldier did get some sleep, which was more than could be said for the officers and the heavy guard that was posted that night. For they had found the local Baluba most aggressive. Not long after their arrival, a deputation of Baluba called on them, and in the unfriendly darkness of the doorway, told them that they were Lumumba supporters, that they intended to march on Niemba and subsequently Albertville, where they would kill all the Europeans, and if the U.N. tried to stop them, they would kill them too.

The patrol was instructed to return to Albertville and arrived back on the 28th. On October 1st, a reconnaissance patrol, under Capt. Flynn, went to Niemba by rail and drove south. This patrol also repaired the bridge at Kinsukulu, but was stopped on the Esa River by a large force of armed Baluba who had dismantled several sections of the bridge. The tribesmen refused point-blank to let the patrol through, declaring that they would have no dealing with "Onee." Precluded by the terms of the U.N. mandate from using force, the patrol had no alternative but to turn back.

With the Katangan gendarmerie in occupation, it was hardly likely that the Baluba would attack Albertville, while it was even more unlikely that they would attack Niemba, since the population was Baluba and there was a heavily-armed and very mobile gendarmerie unit operating in the region west of it. On October 4th, however, a Baluba war party sacked Niemba, burning houses, killing those of their own people who presumably would not co-operate or who could not get away, and kidnapping three Europeans from a passing train.

October was the time of year when peaceful Baluba harvested their cotton, and would sell it to the Filtisaf factory in Albertville for hard-earned francs which would buy them tobacco, salt and foodstuffs. Already the cotton was stacked in bales outside the villages. On the morning of October 4th, a Tuesday, two members of Headquarters Company of the 33rd Battalion, Sgt. Joseph Burke, of Athenry, Co. Galway, and Private Desmond Kearns, Dublin, left Albertville to escort an official of Cotanga, the Cotton Company of Katanga, to Nyunzu, about 35 miles west of Niemba, to pay the cotton workers in that area. A few hours later they returned with the news that the wooden decking had been ripped off the long bridge leading into Niemba over the Lukuga River, and that a large party of Baluba were guarding the Niemba side. They appeared to be holding Niemba, Sgt. Burke reported, and threatened to kill anyone who tried to cross. An hour after this news, the C.F.L. Railway Company (Chemin de Fer des Grands Lacs or Railway of the Big Lakes) informed battalion headquarters that one of their freight trains had been held up by a Baluba war party at Niemba and there were fears for the lives of a Belgian railway official and two Portuguese traders who were on it.

A patrol under Comdt. Keogh was immediately despatched by train to investigate. As the train neared Niemba, women with large coloured bundles on their heads, and their children, who had fled from the village, were seen streaming through the bush, and ignoring reassurances conveyed to them through a loudhailer that they had nothing to fear.

In a cutting just short of the village the train ground to a halt, as part of the line had been taken up, and was soon surrounded by several hundred Baluba warriors. Many of them were screaming and gesticulating and chanting "Cartel", "Cartel", a war cry, derived presumably from the anti-secessionist, mainly Balubakat, Cartel Katangais. With the remainder of the patrol under Captain Richard "Kerry" Sloane covering them from the train Comdt. Keogh and a small party tried to parley with the tribesmen, but they appeared to be heavily drugged, and the only one from whom they could get any sense, an oldish warrior, denied they had any Belgian prisoners. Unable to continue, or to take their vehicles, which had been brought on flat cars, through the bush, and not wishing to engage the Baluba in a senseless battle, the troops withdrew to Albertville on instructions from headquarters. At the station in Albertville at midnight the troops had a quick meal of sandwiches and with reinforcements under Capt. Flynn set out for Niemba by road.

As the Irish now drove towards Niemba from the east, a Katangan gendarmerie unit of 27 Congolese and eight Belgians which had also been notified of the seizure of three Europeans by the Baluba, were converging on the village from the west along the road from Nyunzu. However, it was agreed with the Katangan authorities that this unit would not enter Niemba before the Irish so as to give the U.N. soldiers an opportunity of effecting a peaceful release of the prisoners. Delayed because two of their vehicles, newly-acquired trucks carrying men and supplies, repeatedly broke down, Comdt. Keogh established camp some miles out from Niemba and with the main body of the patrol, pushed on towards the village. As expected, the Baluba were waiting at the bridge when they reached it in the late afternoon. This time a parley produced the admission that the three European prisoners might be somewhere near Niemba, and an offer to exchange them for 100 Baluba held prisoner by the gendarmerie in Albertville. Comdt. Keogh got instructions from battalion headquarters to agree to this, and as it was now dusk he arranged to meet the Baluba at the bridge the following day.

Next morning the Irish were back at the bridge, but there were no Baluba to be seen. They repaired the bridge, and moved into Niemba in tactical formation. Several houses which, apparently, the Baluba had set on fire a day or two earlier, were in smouldering ruins. Only a few buildings in the centre of the village were undamaged. These included the railway hostel, called the Hotel de Chefferie, which from the weapons, filth and food found in it, appeared to have been the Baluba headquarters. The red-brick church on the Nyunzu road had been desecrated, the dispensary wrecked and bottles of medicines and drugs smashed. Shops, houses and native huts had been looted, wrecked and burned. As the troops passed a garage the roof caved in, showering them with sparks. The station buildings also had been wrecked, and bales of newly-harvested cotton torn open and scattered.

The safe in the station office had been rifled, and of the contents—stated to have been one million francs—nothing but the rubber bands remained. As for the train, it too had been looted, part of a consignment of beer having been drunk by the looting Baluba. Of those who had been travelling on the train, all that remained was a half-eaten meal on a table in the crew's quarters—and a pair of ivory dice left lying there from an interrupted game.

The only Baluba in Niemba now, however, were dead ones. Some of them were inhabitants who had been speared to death when the war party struck. They included an elderly native who had worked in the shop at the crossroads and who had given water to the Irish on an earlier patrol. Now he lay huddled in his bed, his stomach ripped open by a spear which lay on the floor beside him, and Comdt. Keogh could not help wondering as he looked at him, how the Baluba had got into the room without waking him. It was soon discovered, however, that a number of bodies on the Nyunzu road had bullet wounds. The gendarmerie had already visited the village. When contacted, the gendarmerie claimed that a reconnaissance party had been ambushed by the Baluba at the edge of the village the previous night and that after firing several bursts the party had withdrawn. This clash had resulted in

25

the flight of the entire Baluba party, and with them had vanished any hope of an exchange of prisoners.

A native railway worker who had escaped the Baluba attack and later returned to the village, stated that in addition to the three Europeans, the war party had taken prisoner 30 villagers and gone south towards Manono. The gendarmerie unit, a heavily-armed party of bearded soldiers wearing wide-brimmed bush hats, wanted to push on down the Manono road, but Col. Bunworth, the battalion commander who had arrived in Niemba at mid-day, refused to allow them, and undertook to have his own men continue the search.

The gendarmerie, however, had not fired their last shot in Niemba. That night they caught four armed Baluba stealing back into the village, and about an hour afterwards when there was a burst of gunfire from their camp, they reported that they had shot and killed one trying to escape. Another, they said, had got away.

During the afternoon, Col. Bunworth had decided that to give the local population protection from militant Baluba and prevent further clashes between the gendarmerie and the Baluba, a battalion outpost would have to be established in Niemba. Comdt. Keogh and he would return to Albertville to fly to Elizabethville and make a full report on the situation to Col. Harry Byrne, Irish commander Eastern Provinces (Kivu and Katanga). The patrol, under Capt. Flynn, would push south to Manono in search of the prisoners, and a section under Sgt. J. Guthrie, Athlone, would temporarily garrison the village.

At midnight, as the Irish were settling down in Niemba for their first proper night's sleep in several days, a radio message was received from battalion headquarters in Albertville, informing them that Lt. Gleeson was flying in from Kamina with his platoon and would take over the battalion's new outpost.

FOUR

Niemba Lives Again

While Lt. Gleeson and the members of his platoon had been looking forward to a change, Gleeson himself had two regrets about the move. The first was that he was going to miss his fellow-officers, particularly Lt. Charles O'Rourke with whom he had formed a firm friendship since coming to the Congo. The second was that he was also leaving behind two sections of his platoon. While Col. Bunworth had been pressing for the return of "A" Company to his battalion, and Lt. Gleeson and his platoon were to be released, it was to be done on a piecemeal basis. Gleeson, however, was assured that the remainder of his platoon would follow him to his new post as soon as possible.

Gleeson and his men may also have been hoping that the weather would be a little less temperamental farther north. Referring to the killings which had occurred in the battalion's area, Gleeson wrote to his wife: "Thank God our only fears at the moment are of snakes and rain. A few days ago I was on the runway, and a thunderstorm broke. I got so wet that money in my pocket turned to pulp. I was trembling with the cold. I was really sorry for myself, as I had no change of clothing. I kept the wet clothes on for one hour, until I got a chance to change. I'll never forget it—it was worse than a bullet."

However, after the change of clothing, supplied by Captain Donal Crowley, the company's second-in-command, Gleeson was right back on the job. This was one of the first tropical storms to lash Kamina base since the Irish had arrived, and the reason the troops could not take shelter from it was very simple. By this time the landings were being controlled by the placing of trucks across the runway: when a plane was authorised to land, Congolese would drive the trucks off. Inevitable, however, in the excitement, and with the noise of the aircraft drowning the noise of the engines, the drivers would flood the carburettors. And so Gleeson and his men got many a tropical soaking.

The flashes of forked lightning were rather frightening at first, but after watching them for a while, some members of Gleeson's platoon found there was exactly the count of 20 between each flash. Trooper Browne, who had soon won over 3,000 francs playing cards, much of it from Belgians, had bought a beautiful Solida II, six-second time camera, with light meter and telescopic tripod, and although the instructions were in French, the Belgian who sold it to him had shown him how to work it. Now, as 24-year-old Private Thomas Kenny and several other soldiers counted up to 20, Browne endeavoured to photograph a fork of lightning.

Although the troops had been writing home almost every day, it was a little while before they received any mail. Now, however, they were receiving letters regularly. Inevitably, of course, there was an odd hitch, as in the case of Pte. Kenny. Occasionally, letters although correctly addressed to him as 57 Private Thomas Kenny (57 being the last two digits of his serial number) went by mistake to 67 Trooper Thomas Kenny in the same platoon. While this was an understandable mix-up which was always straightened out by a simple exchange of letters, the similarity in number and name of these two soldiers was to lead to an equally understandable but much more serious mix-up in Niemba.

Platoon Sergeant Gaynor was especially glad to see the mail arriving regularly from home, since the absence of it made his troops irritable. "You can never guess how precious a letter from home can be," he wrote to his wife Betty, adding that they could always tell when a soldier had, or had not, a letter—if he did not have one, he was depressed and talked to no one; if he did, he was happy as anything. "Now that we are moving out," he told her, "the boys are afraid that we will go on Irish rations and that they will get tea instead of coffee, and miss all the other queer things they have got used to here . . ."

If only for that reason alone, Private McGuinn must have been looking forward to being posted to another area, for though his mother had airmailed him a pound of tea, together with cigarettes, razor blades and soap, it had not arrived. However, with two sections of the platoon he was going to have to stay in Kamina a little longer.

These were the sections under Cpls. Dougan and Kelly and Cpls. Patrick Anderson and Patrick McDonald. Dougan, like the rest of them, was also looking forward to the change. But he too had a special reason for doing so. He was having difficulty getting rid of a cold, was suffering badly from catarrh, and was hoping the change of air would help him. In a letter to his mother, in which he mentioned the cold, he also wrote that they had heard the all-Ireland football final (over Radio Brazzaville) and being a Northerner by birth, he added: "I was glad to see Down winning . . . It is not before our time to win it."

Talk of an impending move had been rife in "A" Company for some weeks, of course, and the general assumption was that when it came it would be to Albertville. When the duties at Kamina had been at their toughest, Sgt. Gaynor had written to his wife: "Maybe we will miss the spring beds and the good grub, but there is the chance that we will be able to lie down and sleep more often than now. The duty here is a bitch's ghost. To tell you the truth, I am looking forward to this new place. The journey is about 400 miles, and I believe we are going by air."

Now, at last the first of them were leaving Kamina. Lt. Gleeson and half of his 46-man platoon were flown out of the base at 1 p.m. on October 5th, spent the night in Elizabethville, and flew north to Albertville next day, arriving at 3.30 p.m. That night they slept in villas occupied by "C" Company on a hill overlooking the Lukuga River, which flows out of Lake Tanganyika. At first Lt. Gleeson thought they were being assigned to the Filtisaf Cotton Factory, but then he wrote to his wife: "I am not going to the factory, but to a place called Niemba . . . It is rather exciting to be on my way." They were detailed to go to Niemba on Saturday, October 8th. They thus had little time to shop for souvenirs in Albertville, but they had already purchased quite a lot both in the "Three R's" Store at Kamina Base and in the town of Kaminaville.

The eve of their departure for Niemba, some of them were to recall, was an almost sleepless one. At midnight the sound of native drums began rolling in from the surrounding bush, and continued all night. The drums, they were told, were being beaten for a death . . .

The patrol arrived in Niemba just as it was getting dark, and Cpl. Jim Lynch noted in his diary that there was a "sick death smell all over the place." By this time Sgt. Guthrie's garrison had established themselves in the railway hostel. Capt. Flynn's patrol, having followed the Baluba south, had linked up with a patrol of "B" Company at Kiambi ferry, and were now in Manono. Flynn's patrol, however, would not return by way of Niemba. On coming to Kiambi they would find the ferry gone and be forced to make a long detour. When, finally, they would return to Albertville, they would have covered 1,200 miles in nine days, in what was to go down in battalion annals as "The Long Patrol". The three European prisoners were not found.

Both Flynn's and Guthrie's troops had buried all the bodies they could find in Niemba, but further bodies, some exposed by torrential tropical rain, were to be a constant reminder to Gleeson and his men for some days to come, of the recent murderous happenings there.

The new arrivals rigged up storm lamps and spent the first few nights sleeping on the floor of the Cotton Bureau. During the week, however, when Sgt. Guthrie and his troops returned to Albertville, they moved up to the road junction—Lynch and one section taking over the hostel, Gleeson, Gaynor and the others setting up headquarters in a bungalow across the way. This bungalow had not been touched by the Baluba as the owner, an Italian trader, had established a friendly relationship with them.

The second day in Niemba, Sunday the 9th, had to pass without Mass, and instead of being a day of rest was a day of hard work for the new garrison. Water supplies had to be drawn from the river, and, of course, all their drinking water had to be boiled. Gleeson wasted no time in instituting patrols, and Cpl. Dave McGrath was detailed to take a patrol down the Manono road. This patrol was notable in that its members were the first to encounter Baluba warriors. Not far down the road they came across a truck which apparently had been owned by Belgians, and saw two Baluba, wearing skin caps, running into the bush.

On Sunday night Gleeson had his first conference in the gloomy lamplight of the Cotton Bureau. He discussed the situation with his N.C.O.s, and as there had been insufficient daylight left in which to retrieve the truck on the Manono road, he detailed a patrol to bring it back next day. However, when the patrol reached the spot where the truck had been, there was no sign of it. The villages in the bush on either side of the road were found to be deserted, although smouldering fires, skin caps, and bows and arrows indicated that quite a large number of people had run off into the bush. Villages vacated in this fashion were to become a familiar sight.

On Tuesday, Cpl. Lynch who was on duty at the station, and some other members of the garrison had an opportunity of renewing acquaintance with 28-year-old Gerry Killeen of Dundalk, who had been transferred from "A" Company to Headquarters Company in Albertville and who was on a train escort returning from Kabalo. Killeen, who had been an Army cook, had followed in his father's footsteps. Soon he would be cooking for the Niemba garrison.

The presence of U.N. troops in Niemba was already having a pacifying effect and the local population were beginning to return. As Sgt. Gaynor wrote home, the Baluba had taken "any of the young men of the villages who would go with them and any that wouldn't they killed. Then they raped any young girls that they could get their hands on and burned down the huts. Fortunately most of the natives fled into the jungle and are only starting to come back now when they see that we are here to protect them." At the same time he assured his wife in a letter on Wednesday: "There is no need in the world for you to worry about anything going wrong or happening to us out here. We take no chances with our health and with the natives attacking us. The locals here are afraid of their lives themselves, and they know that we are their only protection against attacks by the tribes. So they keep on the right side of us all the time." Also referring to the influx, Gleeson, writing to his wife the same day, said: "Since we arrived on Saturday we have cleaned up the village and buried the dead, and the natives have returned to their shacks."

By this time Lt. Gleeson had made his first important contact with the local population when he met a chief from the nearby village of Mehala, who provided two men to help the garrison with their odd chores. Alexis and Moko thus entered the lives of the garrison. Like a few other natives who did some work for the platoon subsequently, they were paid an agreed number of francs each week.

Soon Private Matthew ("Matty") Farrell of Swords, Co. Dublin, the medical orderly, became one of the busiest men on the post, and although he only had a limited supply of medicine and drugs, he did what he could for the steady stream of men, women and children who began coming to him for treatment for a wide variety of ailments. Aged 22, and only 5 ft. 2 in. tall, Matty had almost failed to make the army as he was so short. He liked helping anyone in need, especially children, and once accepted into the Army, he joined the Medical Corps. In Niemba he suddenly found his services in great demand, and while he could not possibly give everyone the treatment they required, he did what he could for those in real need, and let psychology do the rest.

"Every day," Sgt. Gaynor wrote to his wife, "the local natives come here for medical treatment," and he went on to relate how, for some complaints, such as severe rheumatism, which did not lend themselves easily to treatment, Pte. Farrell might prescribe a pill or apply a bandage, rather than disappoint and disillusion those who sought his help.

Very shortly, Lt. Gleeson in a letter home was able to record his progress thus: "This place is lovely and we are getting on fine. The poverty of the people has to be seen to be believed, living in houses where you wouldn't put hens, but they are quite happy. Rich men are known by the number of wives they can buy. I am 'boss' here and I am called 'Chief' by the natives." When writing to his father he qualified this by observing: "They are cute enough. I run the canteen myself, and since they have no shops I sell them a beer or two occasionally."

"We are living on a crossroads in two bungalows, one on each side," he told his wife. "The U.N. flag is flying and Niemba lives again."

Sgt. Gaynor (left) and Cpl. Lynch with Pierre and local children at the river Lukuga on the Sunday, two days before the ambush.

Gleeson and Pte. Jim Cramp, photographed with villagers in the Niemba area.

ABOVE LEFT: Soldiers on the 'dressein', as the supply train was called.

ABOVE RIGHT: Lt. Gleeson and some of his men cleaning their weapons at the cross roads in Niemba. From left: Gleeson, Pte. Peter Donelly, Cpl. Jim Lynch and Pte. Jack Talbot.

Moko (left) and Alexis, two of Gleeson's helpers. At the party they were the star performers on the drums. After this they were warned off by warriors threatening to cut their throats.

LEFT: Gleeson and Lynch see Matafali off to Albertville Hospital.

ABOVE: Pte. Killeen and Gunner Chris Cleary with Feza.

ABOVE: Sgt. Gaynor with Matafali's brother (on his right), the weekend before the ambush.

RIGHT: The day before the ambush. Patrol led by Comdt. P.D. Hogan (centre) gives food to unarmed natves at the bridge over the River Luweyeye.

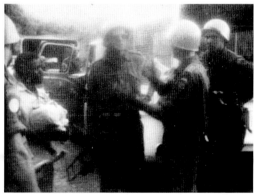

Gleeson and Cpl. Harry Bolger with villagers in the Niemba area. The man in top left skinned the snake for Sgt. Gaynor.

Gleeson with Pte. Daly (beside him) and Pte. Bartley, on Comdt. Hogan's patrol the day prior to the ambush.

FIVE

Down Doom Street

Lt. Gleeson was happy in his new post. As officer commanding Niemba, he was to all intents and purposes, his own boss. He and his men carried out regular patrols on the Manono and Nyunzu roads, and while the work was tough, there were compensations. The bush was abundant with birdlife, and this was a delight to the eye. Ever since his boyhood days in Goresbridge, Co. Kilkenny, he had been fascinated by birds. He had kept canaries and pigeons in the back yard of the local garda barracks, which was his home since his father Michael was the sergeant, and even though the keeping of fowl in the barracks was prohibited, he had on one famous occasion secretly installed a hen in the loft to hatch a brood of chickens. The wealth of colour around his outpost also gave him much pleasure, for as a boy he had also been very interested in flowers, and had been able to name any species one was likely to find in the fields of Goresbridge. Now with Sgt. Gaynor and many other members of his garrison, he was learning to speak the local dialect. "My orderly is teaching me Swahili," he wrote to his wife, "and I am making great strides at it."

They were now comfortably settled in the houses by the crossroads. The trader's bungalow in which Gleeson and Gaynor had established their headquarters was modern and contained many beautiful and expensive woodcarvings, as well as a library, although unfortunately the books were not in English. The library, a hallway-cum-reading room, was just outside Gleeson's bedroom door, and here Corporal Noel Hoyne, the radio operator, had his set. Gleeson and Hoyne, both being from Kilkenny, got on very well together, and when Hoyne received the *Kilkenny People*, he would pass it on to Gleeson.

The one disappointment in the bungalow was the fridge. During the Baluba occupation, the food in this large fridge had gone bad, and all efforts to get the smell out of it failed. At the same time, as Gaynor, who

33

had the good fortune to be allotted the trader's spring interior double mattress, informed his wife, they were living "snug enough". The railway hostel, or the "Guest House" as it was sometimes called, also had been made into a comfortable billet by Lynch and his colleagues. In addition to some furniture they had got from the bungalow, they also had the luxury of a small fridge. Private Malachy Bartley who had a talent for giving a homely touch to a billet, soon provided the houses with curtains and several other simple comforts. Cpl. Anderson's section had now arrived, and was billeted in a house near the station, and Gleeson expected to have the remainder of his platoon in Niemba very shortly.

During the first week or two, the Irish troops added considerably to their collections of souvenirs, with bows, arrows and native drums. But their enthusiasm for these soon began to wane, as they were rather awkward to pack, and they already had some bulky souvenirs, such as the large ebony elephant to which Private Davis had taken a fancy. "I am sick of souvenirs," Gleeson was later to write to his wife. "My latest are bows and arrows—I'll probably drop them over a ditch one of these days."

Some soldiers, notably Davis and Donnelly, were recovering from sunburn of the legs, which had followed a changeover from slacks to shorts in Albertville. It surprised no one that Davis and Donnelly should have the same trouble at the same time. Inseparable friends, they were known affectionately as "The Terrible Twins", a nickname with which Lt. Gleeson had christened them. "We used to call them this," Bartley recalls, "because they would not leave each other's company, no matter who tried to make them, and I think everybody had a go who had any sort of authority."

To encourage his men to take pride in their appearance, and to keep up morale, Lt. Gleeson began to grow a moustache during his first week in Niemba, and urged the others to follow suit. "I am now growing a 'ronnie,' " he told his wife, "and it's coming on fine. All my platoon are copying me, so we'll arrive back looking like Clark Gables." He must have smiled as he added: "Tell me how you feel about moustaches." Sgt. Gaynor also informed his wife a couple of weeks later that he too was growing a moustache, and joked: "Even though I say so myself, it does look well. It is just a sort of Clark Gable affair, but slightly thicker . . ."

Gleeson also impressed upon his N.C.O.s the necessity of keeping

34

the men fresh, smart and alert. In his field book he wrote the following notes for a briefing he held in the hostel:

"Now that we're here a week and are beginning to settle down, I'd like to bring a few small points to your notice. (1) Daily, starting at 08.15 tomorrow we'll have a parade. Cpl. Lynch who is in charge here will be responsible for getting this house on parade and Sgt. Gaynor in the other house. (2) Weapons, shaves, boots polished and uniform—shorts and greens exceptions. (3) Sentries—far too lackadaisical, not alert. Litter—most of us are eating bananas and we forget that the place has been cleaned. Dump your litter behind the cookhouse or somewhere where it won't have to be tidied up again."

Reveille, he told his wife, was at 6 o'clock, with breakfast at seven. The place was tidied up each morning, and the day spent keeping roadblocks at the approaches to the village manned, and on patrols.

On Saturday, when they had been exactly a week in Niemba, Sgt. Patrick Greensmith arrived on the "dressein", as personnel at headquarters called the supply train, with rations and mail. The troops were delighted to get the letters, but they naturally made them lonely. To work off this feeling, Cpl. Lynch visited the red-brick church on the Nyunzu road, and as he later noted in his diary, "was shocked to see what the Baluba had done to the house of God." There was nothing left in the shell of the building but a few broken furnishings. He picked up a broken candlestick, and then tried to put the tabernacle together, but the damage had been too great. That evening, the Rev. John Crowley, Cork, the chaplain, arrived in Niemba and heard confessions in the hostel. Next morning, Fr. Crowley celebrated Mass and distributed Communion on the verandah of the hostel. "The priest had it hard to say Mass," Lynch noted, "as rain was pelting into his face." No one had it easy in Niemba—and it was soon to get worse.

On Monday, October 17th, an agreement was announced in Elizabethville between the U.N. and the Katangese authorities. Under this agreement, the gendarmerie would, as from the 20th, abstain from all active intervention in several stated regions of North Katanga. The U.N., for its part would be responsible for the defence of certain centres in them, and endeavour to pacify the remainder of the regions by intensifying patrols, reassuring the population, keeping communications open, and ensuring their security. The aim of this agreement, known as the U.N. Defence Agreement, was to prevent attacks by Baluba bands on the centres, avoid clashes between Baluba and gendarmerie, keep roads open, and restore law and order. The regions included the Territory of Nyunzu, together with the post of Niemba.

According to Mr. Ian E. Berendsen of the U.N. Secretariat, New York, who was Col. Byrne's opposite number on the civilian staff of the Eastern Command H.Q., Elizabethville, this agreement, the text of which is given in the appendix, was fully endorsed by the Balubakat political leaders who endeavoured to get all their followers to co-operate with the United Nations in this matter. "Unfortunately", he added, "their message did not always get through to the local level."

So far, the roads in the Niemba area had not been seriously interfered with, but very shortly roadblocks were to become the bane of Gleeson's life, and indeed of every soldier in Niemba. In fact the first real roadblock trouble they were to encounter was to occur between the 17th and the 20th, the very day the agreement came into operation.

At 9.15 on the morning of Tuesday the 18th, Lt. Gleeson, Sgt. Gaynor and Cpl. McGrath set off with a patrol for Nyunzu, 35 miles to the west. Cpl. Lynch, who was left in charge of Niemba, and indeed many of the others, were disappointed that they were not chosen to go, as patrols were proving to be the most popular of all duties. However, as it turned out, the visit to Nyunzu was to result in a most hazardous undertaking that would bring Gleeson and several of his soldiers within a hair's breadth of death.

They had been told to make contact with a Belgian priest in Nyunzu to get him to say Mass for them the following Sunday. "The road from here to there," Gleeson wrote to his wife, "was as bad as the one you and I crossed to Achill—away back."

"When we got there, there was a meeting of the Balubakats," he said. Gaynor estimated that there were over 1000 tribesmen in the town. Having made contact with the Ethiopian-U.N. garrison, the troops drove to see the priest, who they discovered was the only European there, and as such was very concerned about the intentions of the Baluba. Even as Gleeson talked to him, some of the Baluba gathered around. They were armed and showed no sign of friendliness.

"When I was talking to the priest," Gleeson wrote, "I heard a lot of shouting, and the priest told us that the crowd was uneasy and had held a meeting that morning and had named seven men for 'Doom Street.' I had a funny feeling that things were not so hot, so I said to the priest, come on I will take you away now. He would not come, but I told him I would come back the following day and see how he was."

On the patrol's return to Niemba, Lynch and the other members of the garrison were brought up to date on the situation. If the Baluba were getting out of hand, as the priest had told them, it was just possible that they might converge on Niemba, and so defensive positions were prepared. "I sincerely hope the 'Cats' don't come tonight," Gleeson added in his letter, "as I would be facing a major decision of whether to fire or otherwise. If they come, they are ruthless, so my conscience will be clear."

The night turned out to be uneventful, but at 6.30 next morning, an exhausted native arrived in Niemba and told them that the priest was a prisoner of the Baluba. Sgt. Gaynor was detailed to take command of the post, and at 10 o'clock Gleeson and Lynch set out with a patrol in the platoon's two vehicles, a Landrover and a Volkswagen pick-up, to attempt to rescue the priest. Having travelled about 28 miles, however, they found their way barred by numerous felled trees. They cleared about five of them, but without proper cutting equipment their progress proved too laborious, so they returned to Niemba, and Cpl. Hoyne radioed Albertville for the necessary equipment.

The priest, as it later transpired was Father J. Peeters, who had been one of three White Fathers in the Catholic Mission in Nyunzu. All the Europeans had left Nyunzu on October 10th, and Fr. Peeters sent his two colleagues to Albertville with them because of the insecurity, remaining on his own to watch over the mission in the hope that the danger might pass.

"But the danger increased every day," he later wrote to Mrs. Gleeson. "Then the Irish came to ask me to go to Niemba for the Mass on Sunday. I said to him (Gleeson) that I will come to Niemba if he will come to take me in his car and bring me back. But I told him also that it began to be dangerous for me in Nyunzu, but I wanted to wait some days to see if the situation might change. Then Lt. Gleeson said: 'I will come back here tomorrow in any case and if the situation will become too dangerous I will take you with me.' "

Fr. Peeters, who excused himself for his poor English, although his description of the incident was excellent, continued: "Very well—I was quiet for a long time. That same day they began to make prisoners (natives) and I was afraid to be taken also. I began to make my valises." Of the following day he said: "I was waiting for the jeep of Niemba—other prisoners were taken and I must not come out of the house. But the jeep came not; I waited till night. . ."

He went on to say that, early next morning, the 20th, "during the Mass many people (hundreds) passed before the Mission with their weapons (arrows, spears, sticks with chains . . .). After Mass I took my two valises and fled to the house of Ethiopians to ask protection and wait there until the Irish will come from Niemba. On that moment I did not know what was happened on the way of Niemba.

"At 9 h I went to the railway station with Ethiopan escort to have a conversation on telephone with Niemba. It was not yet possible. The Irish in Niemba said that they were coming.

"I thought that they will come in one hour—Midday passed. At 3 o'clock again to telephone—'They are coming'—But I heard that the people said that the way was barricaded. I was shut in. It would be very dangerous for a very few Irish to come to Nyunzu if several hundred men were on this way. My hope was rather small."

The Irish were indeed coming, as Cpl. Anderson, who answered the first telephone call, had assured Fr. Peeters. In reply to the previous night's message, battalion headquarters had notified Gleeson that a cutting party would be despatched by train in the morning. The message added: "Be prepared to commence operations on arrival party at Niemba. Road must be cleared to Nyunzu and kept open. Once road open, evacuate Fr. Peeters to Niemba. Return him by daily diesel to Albertville."

When the cutting party did not arrive by 11.30, Lt. Gleeson, conscious of the urgency of Fr. Peeter's predicament, set off with a small patrol in the Landrover. With him were Sgt. Gaynor, Cpl. Michael Costello, who was driving, Pte. Jim Cramp, Pte. Peter Donnelly and two other privates.

"We cleared 25 roadblocks (new ones)," Gleeson later wrote to his wife, "and were held up four miles from Nyunzu by six different roadblocks. We had to dodge them by driving into the jungle, digging most of the way, and out again on the road beyond the obstacles. Just when we got on the road, the party from Albertville were just behind and immediately started to make a path through the trees with power saws. I told the corporal in charge that I was going into Nyunzu, and he should follow when he was ready."

Describing their entry into Nyunzu to his father, Gleeson wrote: "All types of smoke and smoke signals and loud roars were heard ahead of us, and the situation didn't look at all healthy. I was, however, determined to get through despite everything. To be honest, I was more afraid of going back as the road we came was certainly dangerous from all points of view.

"We came to a road near a village and not a soul could be seen. We entered Nyunzu and were halted by about 300 Balubakats, and only for an Ethiopian officer, I would say our chances of getting out would be slim. He was having great difficulty convincing the leader that I was not a Belgian officer, but ONU."

Gaynor described their entry in the following terms to his wife: "When we saw the size of the fallen trees, we knew that they could only be shifted by large forces of well-equipped men. But with a lot of sweat and good planning and good driving, we were able to get off the road and cut our way through the jungle, and when we got into town the Balubas were astonished as they thought no one could get past 37 roadblocks."

Gleeson, realising their extremely dangerous situation, evidently decided that their only chance was to keep talking, and he wrote: "I brought the leader over to our white Landrover and pointed out the number plate and said: 'Can't you see that registration is a Dublin one and not Belgian?' At this stage they were really mad for a row and I began to feel for the trigger of my automatic. I looked round to see how the lads were doing, and I was glad to see a sergeant and a big corporal in firing positions, all waiting for a massacre."

"They wanted to kill the seven of us," wrote Gaynor, "but decided against it when they realised that if we opened fire on them that they could not get near us."

"I said to myself I would get the priest out and blow as fast as I could," Gleeson continued. "Indeed, I had fears we would never get out . . . I was worried about a second jeep-load of my soldiers who were following me behind with the power saws to clear the roadblocks. I noticed a whole lorry-load of madmen moving on the road towards Niemba and began to fear for the safety of the lads."

The cutting party, under Acting-Sgt. John Reilly and Cpl. Anderson were just as worried about the men in Nyunzu. As they were clearing the last obstacle, about two miles from Nyunzu, they came face-to-face with the Baluba. To proceed would have meant a battle, and that would have ruined whatever chance Gleeson's party had of getting out of the town. "Sensibly enough," Gleeson was to reflect, "the lads turned the cars and went back. One shot from them would have sealed our fate."

Remarking that the blue beret meant nothing to the Baluba in Nyunzu, Gleeson told his wife that it took a good five minutes to get to where the Ethiopian house was, "though we were just outside it."

The first indication Fr. Peeters had that the Irish were near, was at 5 o'clock, when, as he wrote to Mrs. Gleeson, "There happened something. The Ethiopians mount in their lorry going in the direction of Niemba. A few minutes passed and they came back escorting the Irish jeep with five or six men. They were all dirty, in sweat and very tired. The jeep was full of spades, shovels, picks, axes, saws and chains, all tools to open the way."

Wrote Gaynor: "He was 26 years among these people, but he really cried like a child when we took him out."

"There were not many place in that little jeep," continued Fr. Peeters, "but Lieut. Gleeson would take also the Mass box with the necessary to say Mass. The Ethiopian lorry escorted us for two miles. There the way was blocked. For a distance of half a mile 6 trees were cut along the way. No vehicle could pass. But the Irish had cut a way through the bush to go around the obstacle. The lorry could not follow us and went back to Nyunzu."

As Gleeson observed: "The Ethiopian officer was not anxious to go too far, as he had his own worries."

Meanwhile in Niemba, Cpl. Lynch became very worried when darkness fell and there was no sign of the patrol. At 7.15 p.m. the cutting party returned. At 7.30 p.m. Lynch notified battalion headquarters that there was still no sign of Gleeson's party. However, it was on its way.

"The darkness was fallen," wrote Fr. Peeters, "The tools were fastened outside and inside; each one choose a little place with a packet on his knees; I was before with the driver and the Lieut. Gleeson, each one a valise on his knees, and we could start. For a distance of 10 miles more than 30 trees were cut to block the way—they had to saw and cut them and pull in the border of the way. We passed several little villages but everywhere it was very quiet. I think that the men were elsewhere: they were convinced that this way was definitely blocked, and they were working on another way—a very luck—They could not believe that a few men could clear away 30 trees—The Irish did it! And so we came to Niemba about 8 o'clock."

It was, in fact, 8.10 p.m. when they returned from Nyunzu, to the great relief of all concerned.

"I hope I never see the place again," Gleeson told his wife. "I was congratulated by Col. Bunworth and they attribute the rescue of the priest a great feat."

"After supper," wrote Fr. Peeters, "we go to sleep. Lieut. Gleeson gave me his own chamber for the night." He was also given the most comfortable bed on the post—Sgt. Gaynor's spring interior mattress.

SIX

Tension Mounts

The following day, Friday October 21st, was a red letter day in Niemba.

That morning, Father Peeters celebrated Mass on the verandah of the "Guest House" at seven o'clock, Lt.Gleeson, as he put it, "having the honour to serve my Mass, an example for his comrades." Later Fr. Peeters went with Cpl. Lynch and Cpl. McGrath to see the church, and when they returned, Comdt. Keogh had arrived from Albertville to pay the garrison. He had good news—the long-rumoured rise in the U.N. allowance had finally come through, and was retrospective for a period. Each man received 763 francs.

While there was little in Niemba or anywhere else in Katanga on which the troops could spend their money, many of them were saving for special reasons, and the rise was, therefore very welcome.

Private Farrell, the medical orderly, for instance, was hoping to become engaged to his girlfriend Emer, when he went home. The extra money, therefore, would come in handy when it came to buying a ring.

The story was much the same with the remaining section of the platoon which that day moved with its parent company from Kamina base to the town of Kaminaville nearby. By this time duties at the base had become rather monotonous and Cpl. Dougan had informed his mother that he was "learning the native language and French to pass the time." He also wrote regularly to his girlfriend Sissy, and since he too was saving up to get married, the rise in pay was more than welcome.

Private McGuinn, still without the tea his mother had posted him as it had got lost in transit, never to be found, was now pre-occupied with thoughts of his wife Bridget, who was expecting a baby. He would be home in January in time for the birth, and he was hoping the child would be a boy.

Cpl. Kelly also was looking forward to a similar event towards the end of January, and he too was hoping for a boy. He already had two daughters, Elizabeth and Caroline, and had sent toys to them on Caroline's first birthday. He had also sent a card on which he wrote to his wife: "When she looks back on this card 16 years from now Lil, she will know that this was daddy here in the Congo."

Both babies were in fact boys and were named after their fathers.

Trooper Fennell was unable to get a proper birthday card for his sister Susan's 16th birthday, even in Kaminaville, but he sent her a black and red headscarf, together with one for his mother. He, perhaps, had a better reason than anyone for rejoicing at receiving the increase, since he had lost his wallet at the base. Yet as he said in a letter to his parents, he did not mind the money so much, it was more the photographs of his family that he hated losing. As it was, he managed, and with the in-born ability of the Irish to strike a good bargain, to buy all the presents he needed, including a handbag for his mother for £3—£3 less than the price originally asked !

That weekend Fennell and his friends saw a local wedding, of which he wrote: "I never saw anything like it. The bride had a costume just like at home, but the bridegroom was wearing a leopardskin around him, and he had nothing on his feet. I would love to have had a camera and taken a few snaps."

Probably the only soldier in the company who was well off enough not to be unduly excited by the rise, was Trooper Browne. Some of his friends estimated that his total winnings by this time were in the region of 5,000 francs, although he had spent much of the money purchasing his camera, souvenirs and presents to take home. He had also spent some of his winnings on presents for friends in the platoon. Ten little Congolese boys who, at the base, had "adopted" him as their friend and guardian, had never gone without a few francs either.

All the soldiers in the section were looking forward to re-joining their platoon. None of them had been in Niemba, although some of them had passed it once when escorting a trainload of Belgian soldiers from Kamina to Alberville for repatriation through Ruanda-Urundi. Train guard duties, like other patrols, were popular in Kamina. Often they would pass large numbers of tribesmen, and referring to one such sighting when on train guard duty, Fennell wrote home: "We met a couple of thousand of Balubas on the way, but we had no trouble with them. They were armed to the neck. They had clubs and rifles and bows and arrows, but they liked the Irish very much, thanks be to God." He added that he was having a good time and did not care how many months he had to do.

In Niemba that night, members of the garrison celebrated in the only manner which was open to them in their outpost—they spent a few francs of their back money on a beer or a coca-cola.

Fr. Peeters returned to Albertville with Comdt. Keogh, but while Gleeson had expressed the hope that they would never see Nyunzu again, some of his men found themselves back there on Saturday. An escort under Lynch had to accompany the "dressein" into the town with food supplies for the Ethiopians, and on arrival at the station, found the Baluba to be as hostile as ever, one big fellow giving them an exhibition of how he would cut them up. The Ethiopians were so delighted with the food, that they presented the escort with two cases of Simba beer, although as bottles were scarce, they wanted the beer to be consumed there and then. However, Lynch and his men preferred to have their beer in a more congenial atmosphere and politely promised to return the empties at the first opportunity.

The Nyunzu affair was the first real trouble the platoon had encountered. In and around Niemba things had been fairly quiet.

Once the sentries had been alarmed to see what appeared to be lighted cigarette ends of someone spying on them from the darkness. But it was a false alarm—they discovered that the lights were caused by nothing more than fireflies. At night the troops would see the campfires burning in villages to which the inhabitants had returned, and sometimes they would sit around a campfire themselves, as Niemba became a rather cheerless place after dark without electric light. By this time they had got well used to the sounds of the bush which they had found rather strange at the start. Now they were beginning to "read" the sounds of the night; to tell, for example, if someone was approaching, merely by the noise of the bullfrogs and the crickets.

The threat from Nyunzu would have been enough in itself to keep Lt. Gleeson and his men occupied in the ensuing days, but now came signs of trouble from another direction.

Gleeson and Gaynor were doing much of the driving themselves, simply because they liked doing it. Gaynor, being such a keen motorcyclist, missed all the driving he did back home as part of his normal day's work, and Gleeson, having bought his first car, a new Austin A 40, the previous November 8th, still found a thrill in taking the wheel. Indeed, driving had been the subject of many a chat between Gleeson and his friend O'Rourke at Kamina. "He used to tell it against himself," O'Rourke afterwards wrote to Mrs. Gleeson, "and he always said to me 'Never teach your wife to drive.' He explained that he tried many times to teach you, but that you learned only when he had gone—from a neutral source. He enjoyed telling this . . ."

So it was that on some patrols Gleeson took the wheel himself, and he was driving when they first spotted signs of trouble on the Manono road. "Today," he said in a letter to his wife on Saturday, October 22nd, "another episode with the Balubas."

"I drove a U.N. van towards Kiambi, on the Manono road," he said. "I went out 30 miles and there before us on the bridge were the 'Cats' destroying the bridge. They flew when they heard the car approaching, but I took all their tools and caps (dead cat skins) and turned my van and came back to report to H.Q."

Monday the 24th was United Nations Day, but in Niemba it was a normal working day, and provided another encounter with the Baluba. As Cpl. Lynch noted in his diary, they were patrolling the Manono road and about 40 kilometres down, natives tampering with a bridge ran into the bush on their approach, leaving bicycles. Gleeson also mentioned this incident in a letter to his wife the following day. After describing how his troops spent each day manning the roadblocks at Niemba and carrying out a daily patrol of 30 miles, he wrote: "Yesterday on the road to Kiambi they met six Balubas and in their hurry to get away they left their hats and bikes behind. I am getting used to their antics now, and they don't worry me any more."

Tuesday morning saw the start of the rainy season and as Gleeson wrote: "I woke to the sound of loud thunder and rain. You could not imagine what it was like. My room is looking into the road and from my bed I can see the roof of the house opposite. It was beautiful to see the rain coming down off the zinc roof. There is a beautiful palm tree just beside the house opposite and it is nice to transfer your gaze from it to the roof . . ."

This was the first of many tropical storms they were to experience in Niemba, and as Gaynor told his wife: "You could never imagine how severe one of these storms can be." Of one storm a few days later, he wrote: "There was thunder and lightning that would put the fear of God in any man. And the rain was so heavy and strong that it really cut the stone out of the road. I am sure that more rain fell here in a few hours than fell during the past few bad months at home."

The Tuesday of the first really bad rainstorm, Gaynor wrote his letter as he lay in his pyjamas trousers on his bed. Two coloured photographs of his family taken at the aerodrome before he left home and sent on to him by his wife were on a table beside him, and he observed: "The photograph I have of you shows the top of your head, and very little more, so please send me a few good ones . . ." Thinking that his account of the White Father rescue might have alarmed his wife and led her to fear that he was taking any chances of "leaving her a widow" he wrote: "Far from it. I love my home and family much too dearly to do anything foolish like that . . ."

When Tuesday's rain had ceased, Alexis, Moko and two other native helpers arrived to do their daily chores, and Gleeson went on to relate in his letter to his wife how he had given the locals as much of the goods as could be salvaged in the town, "as they have absolutely nothing." He went on: "You have no idea how cruel the world can be. No wonder they are so savage and down-trodden. The villages who don't want to fight are burned and the inhabitants killed—they don't even defend themselves. No one wears shoes of any description, and no raincoats. I was watching Alex come in just now wearing my slacks," and he added jokingly "and really I don't know how I ever got out in them, they couldn't be more 'teddier' looking."

In spite of what Gleeson had said, the activities of the Baluba were beginning to worry him, as he continued: "On guard at night the sentries are now getting tense and the strain is beginning to tell. Our crossroads are a main point on the road to Albertville, and the boys from Kiambi and Nyunzu will have to come this way if using transport, but I don't think that is their intention as the road to Nyunzu is blocked and the bridges are down on the road to Kiambi."

He related how the previous night (Monday) a sentry came into his room and told him in a frightened voice: "Sir, Sir, they're here, will I call the lads?" He went on: " NO I said, getting into my pants and boots.

"I went outside and looked everywhere and not a thing in sight. They are beginning to confuse sounds of dogs and other animals with the cries of the Balubas. I went back to bed and placed a chair against the door and went to sleep. All is well this morning."

Next morning, Wednesday, October 26th, things were not so well, and Gleeson had rather more startling news to relate: a sentry had shot a Balubakat scout. "I was down at the station visiting the sentries there," he wrote, "and I usually walk back along the line for exercise, when I heard firing breaking out. I ran all the way back and there to my horror I saw a native being carted in. The whole matter had to be reported."

The incident occurred at 10 a.m. and was described by Gleeson in his report to headquarters in the following terms: "I rushed to the scene of the shooting and learned that one of the sentries on the Nyunzu roadblock fired at an escaping Balubakat and shot him. The Balubakat was conscious and received first-aid treatment. The wound itself would appear to be a flesh wound in the skull. I questioned the sentry and he told me he was aware of his orders not to shoot except in self-defence. He became suspicious when he saw 'Balubakat' and 'Nyunzu' written on his identity card. While the sergeant was being sought, the Balubakat made to escape, but he was told by the sentry to remain where he was. He ran away and was pursued by the sentry. The sergeant came and one man made a run to cut off the retreat of the escaping Balubakat and the sergeant shouted orders NOT to fire. The sentry didn't hear this order as brick buildings separated him from the sergeant. He now admits he fired two bursts over the head of the Balubakat and one shot accidentally hit him. He says he got confused when he saw the Balubakat escaping and thought the best means of halting him was to fire over his head."

Having pointed out that the soldier in question was very young, Gleeson continued: "The wounded man's name is Kakuli Matafali, and he lives in Benge—this village is mid-way to Nyunzu and is deserted at the moment. The inhabitants, I hear, have gone to Nyunzu and are strong Lumumba supporters. The wounded man in question is, in my opinion, a Balubakat scout."

Matafali had come up to the road barrier cycling very fast and when stopped, refused to produce his identity card, which the sentries could see sticking out of his shirt pocket. The sound of the shooting had spurred the garrison into action. Cpl. Hoyne who had been at his wireless set, had grabbed his rifle and run out to give chase. Cpl. Lynch and others in the vicinity also had reached for their weapons and run out to see what the trouble was. The wounded man was carried into Gleeson's bungalow, and Lynch, who had experience as a medical orderly, and Farrell, gave him first-aid treatment. Later, as Gleeson informed his wife, "two doctors have arrived and the lad is okay. He is going back to Albertville." Matafali was treated by Comdt. James Burke, one of the battalion's medical officers, and an Italian doctor from Albertville, and taken to hospital there. Gleeson wrote next day that he heard he would be in hospital for three weeks, adding: "His brother came today to collect his bike and I gave him two packets of sweets to keep him happy." Obviously relieved that Matafali was not seriously injured, he went on to say that he had got in huge stocks of stuff and his room looked like a shop more than anything else. He had started that day selling to a local chief to get rid of surplus stock. "I told him that toothbrushes were wonderful for cleaning teeth, so he bought a few. I was afraid there would be trouble in the village on account of yesterday's shooting, but thank God everything is okay."

Gleeson had also discussed the Matafali incident with his commanding officer, Col. Bunworth and had expressed his concern that it had happened. However, while Col. Bunworth had told him he too was sorry it had happened, not to worry as it was now over and done with.

SEVEN

The Drummers are Warned

Normality once more returned to Niemba, and life continued as before, the Irish continuing their patrols, feeding the hungry, treating the sick and burying the dead.

When Dr. Burke came out to see Matafali, he also treated many local people, including a child with an extended stomach who, among other things, was suffering from malaria. The result of the child's treatment— an enema applied externally—was quite impressive and people were very pleased indeed.

A few days later, the garrison also saved the life of a 12-year-old girl. Cpl. Hoyne had taken a stroll down through one of the deserted native villages on the Nyunzu side of Niemba. Near a hut on the edge of the bush he saw a girl sitting on a small crude home-made wooden chair. As he approached, she started edging the chair towards the doorway of the hut, and assuming that her parents were there, he moved on. However, when he came around that way again and she was still trying to get into the hut, he realised that she was physically handicapped and in need of help. She was very scared of him at first, but he allayed her fears by giving her some sweets. He now discovered that the hut was no more than a henhouse, she was like a skeleton, and was paralysed from the waist down. With the few words of the local dialect which he knew he gathered from her that she had been there since her parents and the other villagers had fled from militant Baluba and would have starved to death but for the fact that she was able to drag herself over to an odd mango fruit which fell from a nearby tree. She was now suffering from severe malnutrition, and as Hoyne observed "there wasn't a pick on her", and she was very weak. Hoyne immediately went back to the cookhouse, got bread from Killeeen, and a mineral from his billet, and gave it to her very slowly. When he reported the matter, Lt. Gleeson told him to fetch her and they would see what they could do for her.

Hoyne, Cpl. McGibney and a few others then brought her up to the houses at the crossroads by sliding poles below the bottom of the chair and carrying her shoulder high.

It was obvious that the girl needed to be cleaned, clothed, fed and generally well cared for if she was to be restored to health, and she was now in the right hands to receive all the attention she needed. The soldiers of Niemba took the poor little wretch to their hearts and lavished on her all the care and affection they could bestow.

When she found herself among so many, however, she was at first very timid. So they set about making her hut habitable, and having washed her, dressed her with some nice flowery material which they salvaged, and given her a bed of Army blankets, they left her back to what to her was home.

Feza—as she told them she was called—became a special patient of the medical orderly, Farrell. In common with many of the others, he frequently slipped down to the hut to see her and take her tit-bits of food, and in a letter said that if it had been possible to take her home with him he would have done so. The troops gave her money, which she tucked away in a knotted handkerchief. Efforts to locate Feza's family, or get any of the local people to take her in, failed. Gleeson went down to a village on the Sunday to see the chief about her, but as he later wrote to his wife: "They had a pow-wow, but they would not take her. I sent through a very tearful message to Albertville. So far I have no news from there. I will tell you the sordid details when I go home." However, Fr. Crowley arranged for her to be placed in the care of the White Sisters, and she was taken into Albertville.

"Maybe," Sgt. Gaynor wrote to his wife, "we will have to pay for her there (at the hospital) but there are nearly 40 of us and it won't cost that much. Anyway, the money here is no good for anything. There is nothing to buy with it."

Serious thought was given at one stage to the possibility of having Feza brought back to Ireland for treatment in the Rehabilitation Centre in Dun Laoghaire, but U.N. transport could not be used for such a purpose, and the idea was abandoned. Members of the battalion, particularly Fr. Crowley, visited her frequently in hospital.

The troops also had been feeding an old woman who had been left behind in the first village on the left, down the Manono road. While she did not ask for food, she came around regularly and was always given something to eat. One day, however, she failed to make an appearance, and on looking for her, they found she was dead. They buried her in a simple grave at the back of the village.

While the finding of Feza towards the end of that week gave the troops an interest and helped to ease the strain on their nerves which had resulted in the shooting of Matafali, the activities of the Baluba tribesman to the south and west were still very much on their minds. It was probably for this reason that Lt. Gleeson encouraged the men to hold a party in his house.

"I have Donnelly, Clancy Barracks barman here, and he asked me to organise a party in this house," he told his wife. "I was delighted to give him the okay. The party was organised for Saturday night, and the priest, Fr. Crowley, and eight men from H.Q. were invited, plus the men from the two other houses. The star performers of the drums were our native workers, who were also invited."

Fr. Crowley, when asked if he minded their having a party that night, agreed that it would be good for morale, and added that he would go along to it when he had finished hearing confessions. The function took the form of a campfire concert, held partly under the verandah of the bungalow. All except those on sentry duty attended and it was a great success. A local chief, who accepted an invitation to attend, composed a special drum tune in Gleeson's honour. As Lynch noted in his diary, even the priest sang a few songs for the lads

Gaynor recited his party piece, "Dangerous Dan McGrew" while Gleeson sang his favourite song. This was so catchy that the men were to apply its name to their refreshments from then on. It was called "Johnny Jump Up", a song Gleeson had picked up as a boy on holiday at his grandmother's place in Maryville, Knockraha, Co. Cork. It was a song that went on and on, having 13 verses and a rousing chorus, but as Hoyne recalls, "It was real jolly, and just the thing to keep a party going. You could listen to it four times in one night and still like it." It began:

> *"I'll tell you a story that happened to me*
> *When I went down to Youghal for a day by the sea,*
> *The day being so hot, and the sun being so warm,*
> *Says I, I'll have a pint, it will do me no harm.*

So into the pub for a bottle of stout,
Says the barman, I'm sorry, our beer is sold out,
Try a whiskey, a Paddy, ten years in the wood,
No, says I, I'll try cider, I heard it was good . . ."

Then followed the chorus:

"Oh never, oh never, oh never again,
If I live to the age of a hundred and ten,
For I fell on the floor and I couldn't get up
After drinking two pints of Johnny Jump Up."

The troops would join in the chorus with gusto, and then would sit back and wait for more, each verse being funnier than the one before. About six verses later, Gleeson would be singing.

"The next man I met down at Youghal by the sea,
Was a cripple on crutches, and he said to me,
I'm afraid of my life I'll get killed by a car
Would you help me along to the Railwaymen's Bar.

Well after two pints of cider so sweet,
He threw down his crutches and stood on his feet,
Then he called for two more, and a toast we drunk up
To the world's best porter, old Johnny Jump Up."

Wrote Gleeson to his wife: "Such cheers and claps, I was amazed."

With everyone looking forward to November 5th as the date on which they would have half of their six months service done, a song which had been composed by Cpl. Anderson and Cpl. McDonald seemed especially fitting that night. Called "Coming Home to You", it went:

"I'm away from home my darling,
On a foreign shore,
But when I return to Ireland,
I'll love you all the more,
I volunteered for service,
In a land so far away,
But now my time is finished
And I'm coming home to stay . . ."

Gleeson and Anderson had been talking about home and about pigeon racing, and with his enthusiasm for birds, Gleeson had written to his wife to tell her about his latest "harebrained idea", and expressing the hope that she would back him up in it.

"I hope to go into the racing pigeon business when I go home," he told her. "A corporal here knows all about them. It will mean building a house in the garden as a loft. Every Sunday I will bring them out with us and they will make their way home. I am thrilled with the idea as I used to love to be with pigeons when I was young. That's all in the future. I wish it would come quickly. How I would love to be home again. I often wonder why I ever came away. There is no place like home with you and Celine (his daughter). I am just half-way through my duty with the U.N. I won't feel the time now until I am homeward bound, and then what a reunion. Please God make the time fly."

The party seemed to cheer up Gleeson as well as his men. Next day, when Comdt. Eamonn Quigley, the battalion operations officer, visited the post and took a note of the facilities that were lacking, he offered to have the garrison relieved. However, Gleeson told him they were happy enough and would stay on.

Gleeson's love of flowers caused him to write in another letter to his wife around this time: "Try and sow some lovely Peace Roses down by the railings. They are about 7s. 6d. each and a very good buy, no matter what they cost I love them so will you get them?"

Soon he was to find how difficult it was to sow the seeds of peace in Niemba. It would blossom there eventually, but at what a terrible cost to him and eight of his men. That Sunday, October 30th, the natives who had been working for the platoon reported that they could not do so any more as the Balubakats had told them they would cut their throats if they did.

EIGHT

Friendly Persuasion

A plan was drawn up by the U.N. towards the end of October to bring Mr. Jason Sendwé, the Baluba representative of North Katanga in the Central Parliament in Leopoldville into Katanga to explain to his people more fully the aims and objectives of the organisation in the area.

Sendwé was the obvious person to try to persuade the anti-Tshombé Baluba of north Katanga to be peaceful, as they virtually worshipped him. Not surprisingly, when the secession of Katanga was ended in 1963, and it was split up into three provinces, he became President of Northern Katanga, but following a Left-wing revolt in Albertville, his murder there at the hands of the rebels was reported towards the end of June 1964.

Originally it was intended that Mr. Sendwé would go on an extended tour of north Katanga and take in Kongolo, Nyunzu and Niemba. However, word of the proposed visit reached Tshombé's ears, and he threatened to have Sendwé arrested, if he came, as he was, to put it mildly, *persona non grata* with the Katangese authorities. The United Nations did not put off the visit, but since it did look as though advantage was being taken of the U.N. Defence Agreement to bring Tshombé's avowed enemy into the neutral zone, and the question of Sendwé's security now arose, it was decided that his tour should be more confined.

Thus, as Mr. Dayal announced in his report to the Secretary-General at the beginning of November: "As part of the United Nations arrangements for the pacification of north and central Katanga, and in accordance with established United Nations principles and procedures, the United Nations has arranged a visit to Bukama (south-east of Kamina), Manono and Kabalo of recognised leaders of the populations of those areas."

Mr. Sendwé was flown into Kamina base, accompanied by two other Members of the National Parliament who were also from Katanga but not Bulabakat, and by Mr. Gustavo Duran, of the Office of the Special Representitive of the Secretary-General, who had been largely instrumental in bringing about the goodwill tour. He used Kamina as his headquarters for the tour, and even though it was controlled by the U.N., gendarmerie who were based at Kaminaville threatened to attack his villa with armoured cars. Measure also had to be taken to guard against any possibility of an attempt on his life by the Conakat, or pro-Tshombé Baluba followers of the Paramount Chief at Kamina, Kasongo Nyembo. Blood had been shed in fighting between supporters of these two in May when Sendwé had come to the base to make a pre-election speech.

Sendwé arrived in Manono on November 1st and there addressed one of the largest meetings of Baluba chiefs ever held in the region. This was the second meeting of chiefs which Comdt. Barry, commander of the 33rd Battalion's "B" Company, had arranged in Manono.

To many of the Irish troops, Manono was now jocularly called "Fear-ó-ní-hEadh", an Irish-language version of the name pronounced "Far-o-nee-ha". This name had originated in Leopoldville in the early days of the U.N. operation, when "ham" radios were used to a certain extent by the U.N. contingents. Gen. von Horn, the U.N. Supreme Commander in the Congo approved of two languages being used temporarily to transmit secret information. These were Amharic (the Ethiopian language) and Irish. The names of places, however, presented a problem. In one message sent by Lt. Col. Ferdy Lee, Irish liaison officer, Leopoldville, by "ham" radio to Lt. Col. Mortimer Buckley, commander of the 32nd Battalion, the word "Fear-ó-ní-hEadh" was used, but the translation—Man-o-no—proved to be rather puzzling to the receiver. After some little delay, however, Col. Buckley did succeed in pinpointing it as the tin-mining town of Manono, which at that early stage was just as strange to the U.N. as a million and one other Congolese towns and villages. Nevertheless, news of this incident soon spread throughout the two Irish battalions, as it was told and retold with some amusement. Soon, however, the code-name "Fear-ó-ní-hEadh" was to be used in deadly earnest.

While Lt.Gleeson and his men had been looking after the needs of the Baluba population to the north in Niemba, Comdt. Barry's company had been looking after the Baluba of Manono. Almost daily since the revolt, Baluba, wounded by Tshombé's gendarmerie, had been streaming into the Congolese hospital in Manono, and the company doctor, Comdt. Beckett, who helped to treat them, watched the number of patients rise from the

15 wounded in the revolt to over 120 in the first week in November.

On one occasion, Captain John Ryan and he brought in 15 or so injured from Kiambi where they had sought refuge. But not all of Dr. Beckett's patients were warriors. Planes had attacked Baluba villages, setting them on fire, and he was also treating people like the 10-year-old boy who was brought to him with phosphorous still smouldering in burns in his leg.

Two days after the revolt, Mr Andre Shebani, the Balubakat representative for the area in the Provincial Parliament, who had been detained in Elizabethville, returned to Manono, and it was hoped that he would have a stabilising influence on the local Baluba.

A meeting of chiefs from the Manono area was arranged by Comdt. Barry on October 23rd. About 10 chiefs came to the town on that occasion, to be entertained by the company, and through an interpreter, enlightened on the task which the United Nations was trying to do.

The Sendwé affair on November 1st, however, was a much more elaborate one. No fewer than 26 chiefs, their wives and witch doctors, converged on the town from a wide area, to hear Sendwé's peace message, and the United Nations flew in a special consignment of Canadian hams for the feast.

As for Sendwé, his return was indeed a triumphal one. As Col.Byrne, commander of the Eastern Provinces, who accompanied him on his tour, recalled, in Manono as in other centres he visited, "excitement and passionate feelings ran very high. He was feted, garlanded, caressed—he was deified." Thousands of people came to the towns to hear him. They took bits of the earth he walked on, and bits of the jeeps he drove in, even to the extent that some of the jeeps would not go again.

It took Sendwé four or five days to visit the three centres, not the least important of which was Kabolo about 100 miles directly west of Niemba where there had been serious Baluba unrest in the latter half of October.

"In his peace mission," Col. Byrne later recorded, "he concentrated on two points. One was the necessity for respecting U.N. troops everywhere and anywhere. He preached that at length. He informed those people who might not necessarily be expected to understand the U.N. mission of the necessity for respect for the U.N. troops irrespective of the colour of their skin. His main object, of course, was to get the Baluba of north Katanga to be peaceful, not to go to war with the gendarmerie."

NINE

The "Cats" Close in

Whether or not Sendwé's message got through to the militant Baluba of the Niemba area, there was certainly no improvement in the situation there. Towards the end of the first week in November it got worse.

On Monday October 31st, the day after the native helpers in Niemba reported that they had been warned off, Gleeson wrote to his wife: "Today all my local men are gone. It seems they will be bad news if they work here. Alex, my man, came yesterday to tell me himself and the other three fellows are heading off today. It's amazing how they say goodbye—they don't, they just walk away. When Alex was going away I felt the world was indeed a queer place. I got on well with him and he and I were very friendly."

The same day a patrol which went half-way out the Nyunzu road to investigate the reported burning of a village, encountered in another village near the railway line a band of armed tribesmen whose attitude showed that the Baluba in that direction were as unfriendly as ever.

At the same time Gleeson wrote: "I hope everything goes well in the next few weeks. I don't expect trouble anyway, although I am in the hottest spot of the Irish battalions."

Meanwhile Col. Bunworth, appreciative of the manner in which the platoon was carrying out its difficult duties, had been on the radio. As Gleeson mentioned in his letter that day: "The C.O. was on the wireless last night and complimented my platoon on the way we are behaving here. It's amazing the morale that my platoon has." So it was, for as Gaynor had remarked on a letter home, on top of everything else "the same faces opposite you at the table three times a day does not help either."

The fact that they were almost at the half-way mark of their service, was also making the men a bit homesick. On Tuesday, November 1st, Gleeson wrote to his wife: "They say that we will assemble at Kamina for Christmas, and the 32nd Battalion will go first and then the 33rd. How true this is, I don't know. It's amazing how everyone is talking about going home, even though we are only half way, but it is over the brow of the hill and it's all a free-wheel from now on."

Having informed her that his health was excellent, he went on: "I love being here on my own. The visiting officers are inclined to feel sorry for me here, and praise is lashed out, but really if I had to shift again it would be fierce . . ." He added that he had written to Capt. Jack Millar of the Army Press Office, praising his radio programmes ("Dateline Dublin" and "Congo Chronicle") "mainly hoping he'll mention Niemba so be sure and listen in."

Private Davis's thoughts were now also on Christmas and home, and he was wondering in his letters if his mother was going to send him a plum pudding.

Gaynor too was thinking about his family. His elder son Brian, whom he called his "motor-bike man" as he also loved motorcycles, would be aged two on Sunday. He also had written to his wife: "I'm sure the little fellow (Maurice) is fairly big now. Do you think he will be big enough to make strange with me when I come home? I hope not. It is very hard for me to guess what he looks like now because they change so much at that age."

However Gaynor had had enough of Niemba to do him for a lifetime. "I have seen enough murder, misery and filth to do anyone," he wrote. "Since I left Kamina six weeks ago I have been in hundreds of native villages, buried bodies of people who were murdered in the most savage ways, and seen people living in huts that had not a stick of furniture of any kind, with a fire lighting on the floor and no chimney."

"Now I can count the time to go home," he wrote: "We are half-way through our time here. We can look forward to going home and I won't be sorry."

The following day, November 2nd, was, as Gleeson recorded in his daily letter to his wife, "like every other day here—warm and sultry." He went on: "The lads are gone to draw water and I am in the room here on my own, so I will drop a few lines to you. I slept well last night—I have a mosquito net over my bed, and during the night I got tangled up in it. I am looking forward to buying a camera. It will cost 1,250 francs, so if you want any particular snaps, let me know. I had myself taken with a few black women holding loads on their heads."

In a more serious vein, he went on: "I have just sent a patrol down towards Kiambi. The bridges were down the last time we were out." Later in the same letter he reported: "My patrol is back to say the road is blocked six miles out, but I told them to steer around it and keep going. These natives won't scare me so easily."

The situation now had been reached where the Baluba, having demolished the nearest bridge—the 20-ft. long bridge over the River Luweyeye, about 13 miles out—were proceeding to block the road closer to Niemba by felling trees, and cutting trenches across it. And while Gleeson did not scare easily, their activities did worry him considerably that night, and he slept little.

However morning time in Niemba could be beautiful, and as the shadows of darkness receded, so apparently did some of Gleeson's apprehensions of the night before, and he set off with Cpl. Anderson to survey the latest damage and report to headquarters.

Describing the drive in a letter to his wife later that day, Gleeson wrote: "I set off with a corporal (my pigeon friend) to see how things were faring on the Manono road. We by-passed some roadblocks some six miles out from here, and were halted by broken bridges. On the way, Kevin at the wheel, the Landrover mounted a tree-stump. The front axle was 'jacked' up on the stump and back or forward we could not move."

They had been trying to drive around a felled tree when the Landrover became impaled. They stripped to the waist, as it was extremely hot, and started digging and pulling. But their efforts were of no avail. "I became very worried," wrote Gleeson, "as I had visions of being stuck there quite a long time. We clawed at the earth for a while, but in the end I knew we would just have to leave it and seek help. I remembered passing a village three miles back, and off we set for it."

Taking up their guns, they started out for this village, and as they walked, Gleeson started to sing, and he sang the "Campfire Concert"—

> *It was at a campfire concert,*
> *On a lonely western trail,*
> *The singers hailed from lands across the sea,*
> *One sang a song of Scotland,*
> *Of Loch Lomond's bonny banks,*

The other sang an English melody,
It was then an Irish lad stood up,
'I'll sing a song' said he,
'You're country too is beautiful and fair,
But I'll sing a song of my land,
Where the three-leaved shamrock grows,
You'll find no place like Ireland anywhere.'

It was a warm day; indeed, as Anderson recalls, it could not have been hotter. But they soon came to the village they had passed earlier, and there met four men. Although there were three or four children there too, these villagers told them that they had sent their wives away because the Baluba were coming. However, thinking that the Landrover was stuck only a very short distance down the road, the four agreed to pull it off the stump.

Gleeson wrote: "The chief of the village and a few men set out with us as they thought we had just walked a few yards. Before we got to our destination the chief wanted to turn back, but we persuaded him to keep going."

Apparently it was the roadblocks which they came across before reaching the Landrover which frightened them. "They sensed trouble," Gleeson continued, "and they were right." The Landrover had come to grief between two felled trees, and as they started to lift it clear, one of the helpers tapped Anderson on the shoulder and ran. On looking up, they saw a number of Baluba watching them from behind the fallen tree to the south of them. Gleeson and Anderson automatically reached for their Gustaf sub-machine guns, but the Baluba faded into the bush as suddenly as they had appeared, and when Gleeson jumped up onto the fallen tree and asked them to come back, there was no response.

Gleeson decided to take no more chances, and to get back to Niemba with the least possible delay. "After a few pushes and shoves and shouts, we yanked the car free," he said, "and went back as fast as we could go." Short of the village they met two of the children and gave them a lift. Before leaving the village, Gleeson gave the chief 100 francs, because, as he wrote, "they definitely took us out of a difficult situation." He added: "I am definitely finished as regards taking chances and risking my life from *now on*."

"The only road now open," he said, "is the road to Albertville," and he went on to sketch the Kabalo-Nyunzu-Niemba-Albertville road, and the Niemba-Manono road on which he put an "X" and the words "6 miles ambush".

"I was very thirsty after it all," he added, "and drank nine bottles of minerals and one box of grape fruit. I am still thirsty, but grub is up, so I'll leave this letter for now . . ."

Taking up his pen again, Gleeson told his wife: "I heard today we will be replaced when we have six weeks completed. I won't be sorry as we have no water or light, or any facilities of any description. The soldiers are feeling the strain especially now that the 'Cats' are expected."

All of the chaps were sick of the Baluba, he said, and he doubted if any of them would ever volunteer for another six months' service. It is obvious that he too was suffering from strain now, as he went on to disclose to his wife that "last night I was awake nearly all night as I was afraid they would fire across at my house and kill me in bed."

To add to his worries that day, his wireless was out of order, and he commented: "I have no communications at the moment."

"You should write every day," he went on to tell his wife "as you can imagine yourself in a 'ghost town' with 38 others and surrounded by madmen. The place is burned—no friends nearer than 70 miles, and the road and railway line likely to be blocked at any minute. How welcome letters are, you have no idea."

The unexpected arrival of Capt. Crowley, second-in-command of "A" Company, which had now moved up to Albertville, cheered up Gleeson considerably.

When the "dressein" arrived at the station, Capt. Crowley was impressed to see how smartly the sentry snapped to attention and saluted, as it indicated that discipline was good. The Volkswagen with the name of its previous owner, "M. Amarshi Fils" still on the driver's door, pulled up, and Gaynor greeted their visitor.

On the half-mile drive up to the crossroads, Gaynor showed Capt. Crowley a bend in the river where they did their washing and pointed out a big coloured towel on a rock which he said was Gleeson's. He spoke enthusiastically about Gleeson and also expressed the hope that they would be back with the remainder of the company by Christmas.

Gleeson was delighted to see Crowley and was delighted to hear the latest company news. He enquired about his friend O'Rourke, and learned that he just been moved 40 miles north of Albertville to a small town called Kabimba. He also asked about the remaining section of his platoon and expressed the hope that he would have it soon. They discussed the Matafali incident, and the injured man's progress in hospital, and various other things, such as the problem of fresh water and lighting. They also discussed Killeen's cooking facilities, food and mail.

Killeen made a meal for them of rashers, bread, butter and tea and Pte. Malachy Bartley brought it into Gleeson's room to them. Then as they sat at the end of the bed chatting, Gleeson made what to Crowley was a strange remark. "I must have my bed changed," he said. "Why?" asked Crowley. "They know where I am sleeping," he replied. While Gleeson did not elaborate, it seems probable that he was afraid that some of the native helpers who had deserted them might have given the trouble-making Baluba details of the garrison's quarters. Some of the men had become suspicious that at least one of them had been able to speak English and eavesdrop.

Before leaving, Crowley told Gleeson that everyone was very pleased with the work that they were doing in Niemba. At the same time, he told Gleeson that he thought that they had been in Niemba long enough, and in fact drew up a plan to rotate the garrison.

Of the Niemba post, Crowley noted: "Morale very high. Living conditions: houses good. No fresh water. No light. Chaps a bit lonely. Tension mounting . . ."

That night the troops in the "Guest House" sprang a surprise on the rest of the garrison by throwing a party in return for the one on Saturday night. It started at eight o'clock, Lynch was master of ceremonies, and as he afterwards noted in his diary: "A good time was had by all."

Next day, the lack of facilities which had contributed to Gleeson's state of depression was in good part remedied. Following Comdt. Quigley's visit the previous Sunday, Lt. Walter Raftery, the engineer officer, had inspected the post, a lighting set and wiring were flown up to Albertville from Manono, and on Friday November 4th Raftery and a party arrived and installed electric light both inside and outside the garrison's quarters.

As the party completed the installation of the lighting, Gleeson took Raftery down the Manono road to show him the extent of the roadblocks. This time Cpl. Harry Bolger took the wheel. Driving aound the felled trees, they stopped at a wide trench which had been dug across the road. Then, as they examined the trench, there was a shiver in the trees, and Gleeson whispered suddenly: "They're there."

Raftery said he thought it was just the birds, but the he saw a movement and he knew Gleeson was right. Pretending not to notice, they continued talking, but with their guns at the ready, until they could turn back.

Earlier Raftery had brought Gleeson the camera which he told his wife he was going to buy, and had the film developed for him.

On November 5th, in a letter that was to be received after his death, Gleeson wrote: "Today is Saturday and I am in Niemba a whole month today. I am feeling fine and in good shape." He had good news—he was hoping to have a chat on the radio with his friend Charlie O'Rourke in Kabimba.

Just then he was waiting on contact to be made with O'Rourke, and telling his wife "I will give you full information as soon as I finish with him," went on to bring her up to date on the local situation. The roads were now all blocked with the exception of the road to Albertville, he said, and he thought the Baluba would attack Albertville in the next day or two. But he added: "Anyway darling, we'll thrash them if they do come." Just then, however, the words "Guards turned out" sounded and as he wrote: "I rushed out with my gun minus my cap and I was charmed to see the Ethiopians from Nyunzu had arrived. I met the officer recently on a train guard. The lads were delighted to see someone and more especially me. I gave him a drink and he told me that Nyunzu was now cleared of 'Cats' and that his men cleared the road in the past four days. My patrol sent out this morning will now go to Nyunzu to see all that is going on.

"Now I have been on to Charlie and he could not hear me. I will try in the morning at 08.15 hrs. He is in Kabimba—a hydroelectric station, but I am happy now as I was delighted to see the Ethiopians. At least the trouble is now in one direction."

Gleeson had sent a patrol under Sgt. Gaynor out towards Nyunzu that morning and they had met up with the Ethiopians. They had also gone into a village on the far side of Benze, and among the Baluba there located Matafali's brother. They had a chat with him about his brother's progress and had also some photographs taken with him and some others.

Another visitor to Niemba that day was the Italian trader in whose house Gleeson and some of his men were billeted. He was surprised to find that any of his possessions had been left after Niemba was sacked, and took away some items from the bungalow, including the beautiful woodcarvings.

During the week two or three other Congolese had come into Niemba and offered their services to the garrison.

One of these had come from a village across the bridge towards Albertville for medical treatment. By this time, of course, the garrison were being very careful about whom they would employ. However, Pierre, as this man's name turned out to be, was a clean-cut type of person with some education. He said he was an office worker and could type, but would do any odd jobs. He was taken on.

On Sunday, November 6th, as Fr. Peeters later told Mrs. Gleeson, "I had again the luck to go to Niemba on lorry with an Irish escort to say the Mass. We arrived before dinner and again Lieut. Gleeson served my Mass." The White Father also heard confessions and distributed Communion.

Meanwhile, Gleeson and O'Rourke had succeeded in establishing radio contact. "When I arrived from Kamina to this small town 40 miles north of Albertville," O'Rourke wrote to Mrs. Gleeson from Kabimba, "I asked my wireless operator to try and get in touch with Kevin's operator and arrange a conversation between us. The distance was 170 miles with lots of mountains so it was rather difficult to get good communication. However, one morning my wireless operator announced that the communication was good, so I immediately took over the microphone and head-set and I talked to Kevin personally."

"He was in great form," O'Rourke went on, "and I told him I had got orders to relieve him, so he explained all about his position there. I was kidding him about what the senior officers of the battalion were saying about the great job he was doing there, and I said he was setting too high a standard for the poor officer who was to relieve him—he laughed."

During the day, Gaynor, Lynch, McGrath and Pierre went down to

Capt. Crowley visits Niemba on the 'dressein' and Gleeson is delighted.

Col. Bunworth and Comdt. Hogan, arriving at Manono where the Baluba had revolted, are stopped at a road block.

The bridge over the River Lukuga leading into Niemba from the direction of Albertville. After the ambush it had to be booby-trapped.

Gleeson and Father Peeters after the rescue.

Comdt. Hogan's patrol stops at the demolished bridge over the River Luweyeye the day before the ambush. Lt. Stig von Beyer, the Swedish interpreter, surveys the damage.

The five bullet holes in the door of the Volkswagen pick-up.

The Irish-Malayan party that recovered Browne pauses on the road south of Niemba to consult the red-pencilled map showing the reported location of the remains. The two Irish officers are Comdt. McMahon (left) and Capt. Jim Lavery.

Col. Harry Byrne, O/C Eastern Provinces (second from left) arrives in Niemba. Also in the picture are: Lt. von Beyer, the interpreter (saluting), Comdt. Kevin O'Brien, Comdt. P.D. Hogan and Comdt. Malachy Mc Mahon.

the river to see where the crocodiles were caught, as occasionally they had seen villagers carrying buckets of crocodile meat across the bridge. They met several children there, and they showed great concern when, to amuse them, Lynch pretended he was going to dive into the river.

Lynch bought a crocodile skin from a villager for a bag of salt, some of which they had found when cleaning out the "Guest House", and he arranged to collect it on the Tuesday. Later, as he noted in his diary, he was detailed to join a patrol which was coming from headquarters to open up the Manono road next day.

This patrol, led by Comdt. P.D. Hogan, second-in-command of the battalion, arrived in Niemba that evening at six o'clock, and a sing-song was held before the troops retired early so that they would be fresh for the task ahead of them.

That night, Gleeson must have felt happier than for a long while. The electricity was a great addition to the post. His missing section was to join the platoon the next day, the Manono road was going to be cleared of its troublesome roadblocks, he had spoken to his friend Charlie O'Rourke, and could now expect to be relieved fairly soon.

Perhaps during the past day or two, the premonition of death which his wife had voiced before he left, had crossed his thoughts. "One of us," she had said, "won't be here at the end of six months." "Don't be silly," he had told her, and now that things appeared to be taking a turn for the better, any forebodings he may have had, must have seemed remote that night.

TEN

Conspiracy in the Bush

U nknown to Lt. Kevin Gleeson, or indeed to any white man, the fires of hate burned deep in the hilly bush country of Niemba that night. During the month of October, a powerful group of armed warriors, of which the roadblocks on the Manono road were only the first symptoms, had been recruited in the area by the Grand Chief Kasanga-Niemba (not to be confused with Chief Kosongo Nyembo of Kamina mentioned earlier).

The warriors, some of whom were recruited under threat, all underwent a ceremony of baptism, in which they were sprinkled with "magic" water while the baptiser pronounced ritual words which they were led to believe would shield them from gunfire.

Having received the baptism, the warriors were placed under the orders of ex-Premier Sergeant Lualaba who had been given the job of conducting combat operations.

The warriors varied in age from 17 to 60 years, and included Baluba who, before independence and when life was relatively normal, were students, farmers, soldiers and so on.

Among them were Michel Kabeke, a farmer, of Kasanga Niemba; Alexis Mukalayi, aged 17, a student, of Niemba; Stanislas Mwamba (40), a native of Kiambi, Kyomo District, Manono Territory and resident at Niemba, a farmer and ex-soldier; Nufabule Banza (45), a native of Kiambi, Tumbwe District, Albertville Territory, and resident at Kabawe near Niemba, a farmer; and Kamatshala Senga (50-55), a native of Kongolo village, Niemba District, a farmer.

Like many other members of the population, they had taken refuge from the civil strife in the bush, and there, they later claimed, they were seized by bands of Kasanga-Niemba's young Baluba and forced to serve under Lualaba.

Whether or not the leaders of this group or "cartel" were aware of the motives of the United Nations troops in the area, let alone the U.N. Defence Agreement, it would appear, in retrospect, that in erecting the roadblocks on the Manono road, they were taking advantage of the absence of the gendarmerie to consolidate their position, and resented efforts by the U.N. troops to keep the road open. As events showed, they also wanted the modern weapons which the soldiers carried, a desire no doubt prompted by Lualaba's military background.

Consequently on Monday November 7th, when the U.N. troops began clearing the road out from Niemba, a war party was despatched to lie in wait at the dismantled bridge on the River Luweyeye.

The Baluba leaders had apparently decided that beyond this bridge the U.N. should not be allowed to go.

ELEVEN

Deception at the Bridge

Commandant Hogan's patrol set out from Niemba on Monday at the early hour of 5.45. All had been up at 4 a.m. and like Comdt. Hogan, found that the moon was so bright they could shave almost without the aid of electric light.

The contingent which Hogan had brought from Albertville included Comdt. Brendan Heaney, medical officer, and Capt. Sloane, and having been reinforced by about 20 men of the Niemba garrison including Gleeson, Lynch and McGrath, the patrol now numbered about 40 all ranks. They travelled in eight vehicles—trucks, pick-ups and Landrovers. Their instructions were to go south on the Niemba-Kiambi road, clear all roadblocks encountered and link up at Senge Tshimbo with a patrol from Manono under Comdt. Barry at noon. Both patrols were to begin the return journey at 1 p.m. whether they met or not.

The roadblocks below Niemba, however, proved numerous and difficult, and at the first, a large tree, the troops broke their mechanical saw. Farther down, they were assisted in removing another large tree by natives who pulled on ropes to the rhythm of tribal chanting. Some villagers who helped them complained that owing to the activities of militant Baluba, they were left with no market for their cotton, no money, no soap or tobacco, and very little food.

After 6½ hours the patrol had cleared one stalled truck and eight trees from the road and bridged or filled in five trenches, but had only covered about 13 miles. This brought the patrol to the bridge over the River Luweyeye. All the logs, with the exception of two or three, had been thrown into the bed of the river.

Now as the patrol surveyed the damaged bridge, Lualaba's warriors watched from the thick bush and tall grass on either side of the road. Lualaba must have been rather taken aback by the size of the patrol. Here were eight vehicles of soldiers instead of the normal one or two.

Even as he considered this he was also to lose any element of surprise he may have been planning to use.

The patrol had estimated that it would take several hours to repair the bridge, and when Comdt. Hogan reported this to battalion headquarters, he was ordered to return to Albertville, as the time was now well past noon. Before leaving the bridge, Comdt. Hogan and his interpreter Lt. Stig von Beyer, spoke to some unarmed Congolese on the road about 50 yards south of the river. Just then the sentries which Hogan had posted at the vehicles, gave warning that there were Baluba in the bush on either side, and Lt. Gleeson instructed McGrath to inform the O/C while he took some of his men and went into the west side of the road to investigate.

The people to whom Comdt. Hogan was talking, however, said that those in the bush were only pygmies who were running away because they were frightened by the vehicles. Returning to the north side of the bridge, Hogan deployed his men into the bush on each side of the road, McGrath being instructed to contact Gleeson and tell him what the natives had said.

McGrath took three men and followed a path down through the bush until they came to a rocky part of the river where they crossed and climbed up the southern bank. There they turned to the right as they thought they heard someone moving in the tall grass. Instead of Gleeson and his men, they spotted a native lying in the undergrowth. They immediately hit the ground, cocked their weapons and McGrath shouted at him to stand up. On approaching him, they saw that he had a bow and five poisoned arrows in his hand, and his skin cap was lying on the ground. They then disarmed him and brought him on to the road.

Questioned through Lt. von Beyer, the captured man maintained that he was a pygmy out hunting. When asked about the others who were with him and who also appeared to be wearing Baluba headgear, he insisted that they also were pygmies and that the headgear was not Baluba. In the end, Comdt. Hogan decided to give him the benefit of the doubt. He was given back his bow and arrows and some bread, and released. Food was also given to the unarmed natives from the south side of the river, as they said they were hungry. The patrol then returned to Niemba.

In the meantime, Comdt. Barry's patrol was making good progress on its journey northward, from Manono. The Baluba these troops had met were friendly, and had shown them around elephant-trap type roadblocks, with the result that they had made good time and pushed on past Senge Tshimbo to within 34 miles of the bridge over the River Luweyeye. On the return journey they took with them a man from the village of Mukanda who required hospital treatment for a bullet wound in his right ankle, and were given a farewell gift of a chicken by his wife. Later, near the village of Kasempele, south of Senge Tshimbo, the population came out to meet them and the assistant chief gave an address of welcome.

To the north, near Niemba, Chief Kasanga-Niemba was planning a rather different reception for the next U.N. patrol to come down the Manono road.

On returning to Niemba, Comdt. Hogan's patrol found that Lt. Gleeson's remaining section, under Cpls. Dougan and Kelly had arrived from Albertville. Before leaving for Albertville, Hogan came across a member of this section, Pte. Fitzpatrick sweeping out the kitchen, and thinking he had seen him before, inquired: "Where did you serve?" Fitzpatrick, Hogan recalls, replied with a grin: "In the dining room of the Gresham Hotel, Sir," and went on with his sweeping.

Niemba, Fitzpatrick found, was a far cry from Dublin's Gresham Hotel, but he and the other members of the section were happy to be back with their platoon, and Niemba was a welcome change from Kamina. They were allotted a shop—one of two which had been operated by the Italian trader—near Gleeson's bungalow as their quarters, and set about cleaning it out. Some of them had a bottle of beer that night to celebrate their reunion. It was the first time that the whole platoon had been together for four or five weeks, there were now almost 50 of them in Niemba, and indeed Pte. Kenny could not help but wonder what so many troops were doing in the middle of nowhere guarding, as far as he could see, nothing.

Many members of the garrison again went to bed early that night because, as Lynch had noted in his diary, it had been a tiring day. But for Kenny, this was his first wedding anniversary. It was a bright moonlit night, and his old friend Trooper Brendan Dalton called for him in the Volkswagen pick-up and drove him down to his billet near the railway station, where they swapped experiences of the past few weeks over a bottle of beer and a lemonade.

The following morning, Tuesday November 8th, Gleeson was up again early, as there was much to do. He had been notified that Matafali was being discharged from hospital and would have to be met at the station and driven to his home.

In addition he had been instructed by battalion headquarters the previous evening to continue to patrol the Manono road. This mission, as described in an extract from the battalion's Journal of Events, was "to continue to patrol along route travelled by Comdt. Hogan's patrol of 7th Nov.—to see if in time could push a patrol as far as Kinsukulu. No terrific urgency."

After breakfast, the new arrivals resumed the cleaning up of their quarters. In the process of doing so, Kenny came across a small square magnifying glass and popped it into his pocket as a souvenir. In a few hours that glass would be of much more value to him than a mere souvenir.

At about 10 o'clock, it appears, Gleeson called Gaynor and suggested that they should check the position on the Manono road. He asked Hoyne if he wanted to go along. Hoyne, having made his morning check call to headquarters, said he would, and off the three of them went, Gleeson at the wheel of the pick-up. Along the way it began to rain, and before long the red-dust road had become a quagmire. Gleeson, therefore, turned the pick-up and headed back towards Niemba, since to continue with the road in such a bad condition would be to run the risk of getting stuck.

On the way back they ran a wheel of the vehicle over a bright green snake about four feet long which was slithering slowly across the muddy road. They jumped out, and while Gaynor broke off a forked stick and pinned down the snake, which was still very much alive, Hoyne finished it off with a spanner. They then threw it into a bucket in the back of the pick-up. In Niemba, Gaynor took the snake, sought out an old man in a nearby village, and asked him to skin it and make a purse for his wife.

Meanwhile, the members of the new section had been enjoying their first heavy rain in Niemba. Soon the water began to pour down from an overflowing gutter, and after filling their mess cans from it, Dougan, Kenny and Browne took the opportunity presented by the cascading water to take a nice refreshing shower.

71

Gleeson had returned just in time to collect Matafali who had been taken from the hospital in Albertville by Capt. Crowley earlier that morning and placed in the care of an Irish patrol which was escorting a train to Kabalo.

With a patrol of about seven men, Gleeson took Matafali to his village, and there he handed him into the care of his mother. After lunch he would organise another patrol—for the Manono road. Since half his men were still tired from the previous day, he would take the new section which was fresh and in need of a familiarisation patrol.

During the morning one or two soldiers wrote a few words home. Browne had written regularly so his sick mother would not be worried about him, and when she was in hospital had even written to one of the nurses, who had asked his mother for the foreign stamps so that she could have a few. He also had written regularly to his girlfriend, Linda, and the fact that he had a girlfriend did not stop him writing to another Dublin girl one of his pals had told him about, just for the fun of it. He asked this girl what she was like, to which she replied that she was a blonde. He promptly wrote back and asked her if she was a real blonde. Telling his father about the correspondence which followed, he said: "She wrote to me and asked me was I a good-looking fellow, and I wrote back and said she was writing to the handsomest man in the Congo!"

Before going out on the Manono road patrol, Farrell, the medical orderly, wrote a letter to his sister, Ester, at Seatown Villas, Swords, Co. Dublin, in which he said: "Just a few lines to let you know I got your letter okay, and I am glad you and the family are keeping fine, as I am myself T.G. Well, Joseph, (a nephew) still thinks I am still in the plane. I had to laugh when I read it. Well, Ester, I cannot bring home much stuff with me. They will be checking weight going back. I have a nice scarf for you. I didn't buy much stuff as it is very dear out here. The money we are getting is only keeping us in post and a smoke, and maybe a bottle of Johnny Jump Up as the drink is terrible out here."

Farrell had been trying to get Joseph a drum, and after telling his sister that he might be able to get a tom-tom, went on; "I will be looking forward to a few cigs at Xmas P.G., as the cigs out here are terrible. We were supposed to get free post, but didn't . . ."

"Things have quitened down, so we are nearly finished out here, T.G.," he added.

A typical soldier's letter voicing complaints typical of soldiers the world over, its one note of optimism was to prove sadly wide of the mark. Things had quitened down, as he had said, but it was the lull before the storm.

In the expectation that the U.N. troops would now try to open the road for a further distance south, ex-Sergeant Lualaba and his warriors were that morning again in ambush position at the broken bridge on the River Luweyeye, having been instructed by Chief Kasanga-Niemba before they set out: "Either the Irish soldiers will turn back on the road, or else it is war, and you will win or die."

For this patrol there was to be no turning back.

TWELVE

It is War

Having had lunch, the patrol piled into the platoon's two vehicles. In addition to the new section, it included Lt. Gleeson, Sgt. Gaynor and Privates Killeen and Farrell. Private Bartley was to go, and someone had thrown a faded green and yellow deckchair into the back of the Volkswagen pick-up as a seat for him. However, unlike the others, he had had his fair share of patrols in the area, and at the last minute received word from Lt. Gleeson that he would not be going on this one. Thus, with Killeen seated in the deckchair, the patrol moved off. It was now 1.30 p.m. Later, after the ambush, some members of the garrison seemed to remember that a native who had been watching the departure, mounted his bicycle and pedalled off.

As the two vehicles rumbled down the Manono road, dusty again in the tropical sun, the troops who were seeing the countryside for the first time, thought how different were the rolling hills, or what they could see of them through gaps in the thick bush and long grass, to the flat featureless base at Kamina. Near a village they pulled up to lay planks across a trench which had been dug in the road by Baluba, and then they were on their way again to the smiles of several local people with whom they exchanged the customary phrase of friendship, "Jambo".

Gleeson led in the Volkswagen pick-up, which was driven by Gaynor, and also contained Dougan, Farrell and Killeen. The Landrover was driven by Kelly, and in it were Kenny, Fennell, Browne, McGuinn and Fitzpatrick. Since McGuinn and Fennell were the Bren-gunners, their Landrover also carried two Bren guns. After the ambush Fitzpatrick was to report that as far as he could remember Gleeson, Gaynor, Dougan, Kelly and Browne had Gustaf sub-machine guns, although he also reported Killeen as having a Gustaf during the battle. Three had rifles, including Fitzpatrick and Kenny.

The patrol crossed three trenches, laying planks over two and filling in the other. A few miles down the road, they again stopped, and Gleeson and Gaynor went into a village on the left-hand side of the road and came out in good humour. They became serious, however, when farther along they saw Baluba running across the road ahead of them and disappearing into the bush. After a pause to see if there would be any more moves, the patrol continued until a few miles farther on they spotted a number of Baluba on the road. They too scattered into the bush. After another wait, while he tried to size up the situation, Gleeson got out. He carried his Gustaf and according to Kenny it was loaded and cocked. Walking back up the road, he stopped eight or nine yards past the Landrover. He told the men to get out of the vehicles, and asked them if they thought the Baluba were armed. They said they did. Gleeson then turned and went down past his own vehicle towards a broken bridge, 12 or 15 yards ahead. Kenny, who had travelled in the front of the Landrover with Kelly and kept an eye on the milometer, estimated that they were 13 miles from Niemba. He was right. They were at the bridge over the River Luweyeye. It was now after 3 p.m.

The vehicles had stopped on the right-hand side of the road with the front of the pick-up almost opposite the path, running down to the river, which Cpl. McGrath had taken on the previous day's patrol. Having posted Fitzpatrick and Browne on sentry duty at the back of the Landrover, Gleeson called on Kenny to accompany him to the bridge, and Gaynor went with them. Gleeson asked Kenny, whom he knew to have been attached to the Corps of Engineers in Clancy barracks in Dublin, if they could repair it sufficiently to take the vehicles across.

Kenny, after examining the bridge, suggested going down the river bank to try and find a shallow spot where they could drive across. They went west along the river bank a short distance, until they came to a place which they thought might serve their purpose if it were built up a little. Then they crossed the river and walked up to the road on the south side, where Dougan and Kelly joined them. Before going down the road with the other three about 100 yards to see if there were any more obstructions, Gleeson told Kenny to get a shovel and start clearing the scrub down to the spot where they hoped to be able to ford the river. Kenny, his rifle still slung across his back, walked back to the bridge, but on glancing after them, saw them turn away quickly and come towards him. He heard Gleeson saying that there were Baluba coming down the road, and they saw him turn and start to walk backwards. Kenny knew then that there must have been danger.

On reaching the bridge, Gleeson said to Gaynor: "Turn the cars quick." Gaynor and Kelly ran down to the ford to carry out his orders. Gleeson, Dougan and Kenny followed, with the intention of getting into the vehicles.

Meanwhile, Fitzpatrick was observing to his right along the road down which they had come from Niemba, when he saw a number of Baluba moving around in the bush before coming out on to the road to form up six abreast in a sort of military fashion about 100 yards away. They were armed with bows and arrows, clubs and spears. Just then, as Fitzpatrick was later to report, he became aware of Gleeson and other members of the patrol beside him.

On reaching the road Gaynor had jumped into the Volkswagen pick-up, probably throwing his Gustaf on the seat beside him, started the engine, and begun to turn the vehicle at the entrance to the little path running down to the river. At the sound of the engine, however, a large tree toppled across the road somewhere behind him. Then the warriors, led by ex-Sergeant Lualaba shouting the rallying cry "Cartel", hurled themselves down the road towards the patrol, screaming and brandishing their weapons as they ran.

Gaynor, according to Kenny, stopped the pick-up, and jumped out.

The troops were now in a line with their backs to the bridge and facing towards Niemba.

Reported Kenny: "Lt. Gleeson shouted. 'Hold your fire, we have to wait until they fire first.'" They had not long to wait, as heedless of Gleeson's call of "Jambo" the Baluba unleashed a hail of arrows on reaching the back of the Landrover.

Driven back with his colleagues, Gaynor apparently was unable to go forward and around the open door of the pick-up to retrieve his sub-machine gun. McGuinn's and Fennell's Bren guns were in the Landrover now over-run, and Farrell, the medical orderly, was not armed.

The Baluba, Kenny reported, "were now almost on top of us. Gleeson gave the order to fire." About 15 warriors, including Lualaba, were killed, a court would be told, and a dozen others, including Kabeke, Mukalayi, Mwamba, Banza and Senga, wounded.

Only a few seconds had elapsed from the time Gleeson and his men had rushed back across the river, until Lualaba's screaming horde had burst down upon them.

The patrol paused for a moment after firing. Then Gleeson, knowing that there was another band of warriors coming up behind them, told his men to take cover. They took the path down to the river, which McGrath had taken the day before, closely followed by crazed warriors who believed that only if they did not show courage could they die.

As they crossed the river and clambered up the far bank, Kenny felt an arrow pierce his right buttock, but he kept going. Then they made for a rise surmounted by a rock and a scraggy tree, and there, 40 yards from the road, they turned to face their attackers. "The Balubas were lining the bank of the river," Kenny was to report. "I couldn't say how many of them there were. They were only about 10 yards away. They were shouting and Lt. Gleeson spoke back to them."

At that stage Kenny remembers Gleeson being on his left, with Gaynor hunkering beside the lieutenant, while out of the corner of his eye and to the right, he could see Dougan, Kelly and McGuinn. Even as the arrows whistled through the air, Gleeson tried to talk peace to his attackers. With the phrases of Swahili he knew, he endeavoured to reason with a big warrior, on the far side of the river, who seemed to have assumed command. But the Baluba were beyond the stage of reason.

It was now apparent that the troops were hopelessly outnumbered, with up to 100 warriors, including the first band they had seen on the south side of the river, closing in on them through the long grass. Several soldiers had been wounded by arrows, including Gleeson who had been hit on the left shoulder and, Kenny remembers, also in the knee. Since Baluba arrows were usually poisoned, and Gleeson's knee was shattered, his chances of coming out of the fight alive were slim. He knew he was going to die, and turned to Kenny and told him so.

There was, however, precious little time for talk. For as a trial judge was later to recount, "through a shortage of ammunition, the soldiers were unable after a short while to continue the fight."

The Baluba were closing in, Gleeson suggested that they had better pray, and those who heard him joined in a "Hail Mary". Then the warriors rushed them. Gleeson shouted at his men to "Get away", and "Run for your lives".

In a bitter hand-to-hand fight that followed, Gleeson, Gaynor, Kelly, Dougan and McGuinn died in the vicinity of the rise, the words of the "Hail Mary" on their lips. The other six succeeded in breaking through the circle of attackers, and a running battle ensued. Kenny felt a second arrow pierce him in the same place. Killeen, according to Fitzpatrick, fired and told them to carry on. At the foot of the slope, Fitzpatrick turned and saw a young warrior almost on top of him with a hatchet raised in his hand. He shot him with his rifle. As Fitzpatrick was later to report, they found the bush very dense and the grass and weeds as high as their chest, and they could not keep together. He saw Browne on his right, firing his Gustaf. A few yards farther on, also on his right he saw Fennell who had been wounded by an arrow. Coming to a narrow, swampy piece of ground, Fitzpatrick took cover, and saw Fennell run around it on his right.

A short distance from the hill, Kenny also met up with Fennell, who started off again. Then Browne, firing his Gustaf as he ran, came up. At this stage Kenny saw a warrior, who was using a giant anthill as camouflage, about to unleash another arrow at them. Unarmed himself now, except for a bayonet, he pointed him out to Browne, who turned his Gustaf on the attacker.

Thirsty for blood, the warriors were now swarming through the bush searching out members of the patrol. Kenny and Browne also found themselves in a swamp, a rather soggy patch covered with scrub and cane through which long grass and ivy-like leaves entwined themselves. They could hear the Baluba coming, cheering, close behind. Kenny stumbled and began to make a way through the scrub, while Browne, standing to one side, fired at their pursuers. Browne then followed, but Kenny, weak with exhaustion and loss of blood, fell again into the mud and water and could not get up. Now as he crawled farther into cover, Kenny could hear the warriors slashing their way in, and Browne, still firing, moving off ahead and to the right.

Instinctively Kenny began to bake himself with mud, as he had been taught to do in exercises in the Phoenix Park back home in Dublin, and lay dead still. But the hacking came closer and closer, and then the warriors spotted him lying with his face in his left hand, his right outstretched towards his blue helmet. There was silence for a moment as they watched him. Then he felt the sting of a third arrow, this time in the back of his neck.

Moving in on top of him, the warriors wrenched the arrow from his neck and began raining blows on the back of his head with their clubs. But in spite of the extreme agony he did not call out. He prayed: "God be good to my wife and child," and began to say an Act of Contrition. Soon the blows spread all over his body and he became a mass of almost unbearable pain. His right hand was bruised and swollen from the beating, and his left was warm with the blood that trickled from the back of his battered head, and ran down his face in muddy rivulets. He prayed to God to let him die and release him from all his pain. At the same time, the swamp was cushioning his body and helping him to absorb the blows, and he clung to the hope that if he did not cry out his tormentors would think he was dead and leave him.

Suddenly there was a burst of shots, and he knew it was Browne on his right with the Gustaf. The warriors backed away from him, then charged over him towards the sound of the shots. Left alone at last, Kenny waited for darkness and the lingering death which he now believed to be inevitable.

Fitzpatrick, also having sought refuge in a swamp, could hear his attackers all round him. Later he broke cover to go to the aid of Killeen who was locked in mortal conflict with several warriors.

He fired, and the Baluba fled. Killeen joined him in the swamp, but died in his arms ten minutes later. Eight members of the patrol had now died in the battle.

When, finally, the battle died down, the Baluba warriors put 11 of their wounded in the U.N. vehicles, which they somehow got across the bridge, and sent them south to Kiambi for whatever treatment they could find. Then they set about burying their dead. Reports of their casualties were to vary. A member of a subsequent search party reported that he personally saw seven Baluba graves. The wounded were to state in Manono that they lost 10 killed. An unconfirmed report from the local population put casualties at 11 killed and 25 missing, while information gained in Kiambi about a week after the ambush indicated that the bodies of 25 Baluba were buried while another 25 were missing.

From the bodies of their victims, the Baluba took weapons and some clothing of which there was a general shortage in the area. However, they had not accounted for all the Irish. Three had escaped: Fitzpatrick, Kenny—and Browne.

THIRTEEN

Signs of Battle

Having made his mid-day check call to headquarters and being told by Gleeson that there were no messages to send, Cpl. Hoyne had his lunch and rambled down to Feza's village on the Nyunzu road in search of records for an old gramophone they had found. On returning to Niemba, Cpl. McGrath told him that Gleeson had been looking for him to see if he wanted to go on another spin to the bridge. "I'm sorry I missed him," said Hoyne. "I would like to have gone."

Pierre had been pestering Cpl. Lynch during the morning for his pay, and in the end Lynch gave him 100 francs out of his own pocket, for which he got him to sign. At 2.30 p.m. Pierre left for his village to collect his coat as it looked like more rain, and did not return.

Lynch and Pte. Jack Talbot went for a walk in the Albertville direction as far as the bridge, and then cut back to the wreckage of the old dispensary beside the church to see if there was anything else they could salvage for garrison use. They met no one and felt that things were unusually quiet.

As the day drew towards a close, Lynch and his colleagues awaited the return of Lt. Gleeson's patrol. When it was not back by six o'clock, battalion headquarters was notified. At eight o'clock Lynch radioed headquarters that the patrol still had not returned. This, however, did not cause undue concern in Albertville. Gleeson had been later before and it was thought that one of his vehicles had broken down or he had been delayed by roadblocks. The news an hour later that the patrol had still not arrived did cause concern, as it seemed to confirm that the patrol was indeed stranded. As the Niemba garrison had no more vehicles, Comdt. Hogan, in consultation with Col. Bunworth, arranged to send out a stand-by party, under Lt. Jeremiah Enright to locate the patrol and assist it back to Niemba. Lynch was told to expect Enright's patrol at 1.30 a.m.

Meanwhile, there was an air of tension in Niemba. The night was unusually quiet, and not a fire burned in the surrounding bush. The garrison was on the alert and as a precautionary measure grenades were primed. Preparations were made to receive the patrol from Albertville, and in accordance with instructions from headquarters, Lynch had ten men under Cpl. Bolger standing by to join it.

When 1.30 a.m. came and went, and there was no sign of Enright's patrol, Lynch's worries doubled. Two o'clock came, three o'clock and still there was no sign of it. Headquarters was notified that a second patrol was overdue. However, Enright and his men arrived at 3.45 a.m., having been delayed by muddy road conditions and a puncture. Finding that Gleeson's patrol had still not returned, Enright stopped only long enough to have tea and sandwiches and left to look for it at 4.45. With the soldiers he had collected at Niemba, there were now 27 men in his patrol, including Dr. Heaney who had come with him from Albertville, and Lynch.

A mile and a half from Niemba the patrol encountered a felled tree, but with the exception of six trenches which were negotiated in the usual way by laying down planks, no more obstacles were met, and the River Luweyeye was reached at 5.30. It was now light, and having deployed his troops in defensive positions, Enright crossed the broken bridge. There he saw tyre marks, indicating that Gleeson's patrol had gone across. But while Enright's men now worked to repair the bridge, some blood, several empty Gustaf cartridges, an empty magazine and an arrow were found. Enright immediately notified headquarters.

"We continued our search around the area," Lynch reported, "and in our endeavour to find some planking to cross the bridge we cut into the right hand side of the road on the far side of the bridge." There, Lynch, accompanied by four or five men, including Cramp and Butler, found four bodies in the vicinity of the rise. It was now approximately 8.30 a.m.

"There are the lads over there, Sir," Lynch informed Enright, and shouted for the doctor. The bodies were those of Gleeson, Gaynor, Dougan and McGuinn. Sitting on the rise was Killen's faded green and yellow deckchair. Just then, as the troops surveyed this bizarre scene, one of them thought he heard the sound of drums.

Enright assembled his patrol into a close defensive position around his vehicles, and as he later reported, "a man dressed in the uniform of the

Irish contingent, came out of the bush and walked towards us down the road on the north side of the river." The man was Private Fitzpatrick.

When Killeen had died, Fitzpatrick estimated it must have been after four o'clock. There were still occasional bursts of Gustaf sub-machine gun fire. He remained where he was. At about 9 p.m. he heard the noise of jeep engines, and let off a round in the air, but drew no response. About midnight he decided to move into thicker bush. He had then blackened his face and body with mud. During the night, as he hid in the bush, he heard singing and roaring in a nearby village. This presumably was his attackers celebrating the massacre of the peacemakers of Niemba. It continued all night.

In the light of the moon, just before dawn, Fitzpatrick saw that he was close to two native houses and he moved off to try and find the river. On the way he stumbled over four bodies. It took him two more hours to find the road, crossing and recrossing the river several times. Suddenly he heard the sound of jeeps, and hid in some bushes at the side of the road in the hope that the jeeps would come along to where he was. Several times he changed his position. Then he heard oil drums being moved down at the bridge and found Lt. Enright's patrol. It was now approximately 9 a.m.

Shocked, but uninjured, Fitzpatrick was able to tell the patrol what had happened. Lynch took his rifle and 23 rounds of ammunition which he had left from his original 50, and after being attended by the doctor he was given blankets and put into one of the vehicles. At last he was in friendly hands.

However, the danger was not yet over. Some minutes later a new threat presented itself. Considerable movement of Baluba was observed in the surrounding bush, and it drew a warning burst from one of the patrol's Bren guns. Enright reported the presence of the Baluba to headquarters and was instructed to return to Niemba immediately to await reinforcements.

In Niemba, the garrison which now had heard the grim news, watched a woman and two men approach their defensive positions from the Albertville side of the railway. McGrath went forward to speak to them. The woman had come to complain to them that "Onee" had killed her son.

On returning to Niemba, Lynch issued a packet of cigarettes and a much-needed drink of beer to each soldier while they awaited reinforcements from Albertville.

When Enright sent the earlier message that he had found empty shells etc., at the bridge, Capt. Sloane immediately ran to inform his commanding officer. Comdt. P.D. Hogan heard the sound of his heavy boots pounding down the corridor and then Sloane burst in to announce: "Trouble Sir . . . at the bridge." Hogan and Comdt. McMahon, who was sleeping in the same room, jumped up and roused the C.O. whose room was nearby.

As the members of Enright's patrol carried out their grim search, Col. Bunworth held a conference with his staff at which it was decided to reinforce the Niemba garrison as a matter of urgency, with as many men as possible under the command of Comdt. Hogan, who was familiar with the area. The strength of the reinforcements was largely determined by the amount of transport available—which was rather limited—and virtually all the unit's vehicles were put at Hogan's disposal. McMahon volunteered to go, and Hogan requested that Company Sgt. Keane should also be sent. At 9.50 a.m., Hogan left Albertville to set up a forward headquarters in Niemba. He had a patrol of 70 all ranks, including McMahon, Capt. Crowley, Fr. Crowley, Raftery, the engineer officer, von Beyer the interpreter, and Keane.

It had been decided at the conference that Col. Bunworth would meet Col. Byrne, who, accompanied by his operations officer, Comdt. Kevin O'Brien, was on his way to Albertville on a tour of inspection, and inform him first hand of the situation and discuss further action. It was Col. Byrne's intention to visit also Manono, Kabolo and Nyunzu. When his white Beaver plane landed in Albertville, however, Col. Bunworth informed him: "Sorry Sir we have no guard of honour for you. I'm afraid we have lost some of our men." Byrne thought at first that a truck had crashed. He asked: "How?" Bunworth replied: "I'm afraid they've been killed by Balubas in an ambush."

After discussions, Col. Byrne decided that the unit should be allotted aircraft and ordered two helicopters to be flown from Kamina for immediate use in evacuating wounded and dead. He also decided that full and accurate information should be continuously made available on such vitally important matters as names of dead, condition of wounded, progress of the search, and so on. As a result, rumours of further attacks which were soon rife, were quickly scotched, and demands for accurate information from U.N. provincial headquarters at Elizabethville met with least possible delay.

Col. Byrne directed Col. Bunworth to supervise matters at Albertville on his behalf, while he cancelled his tour of inspection and decided not only to go to Niemba but to Manono to demand an explanation of the attack from Mr. Shebani, the local Baluba representative.

FOURTEEN
"A" for Ambush

Elsewhere on Tuesday, the day of the ambush, it had been a day like any other day.

In Dublin that afternoon, Mrs Imelda Gleeson and her daughter Celine had gone shopping in Terenure, Dublin, and in McGuirk's shop had bought a Christmas card for Celine to send to her daddy. An aunt of Mrs Gleeson's in Rathgar, Dublin, was preparing to send him a Christmas cake. In Goresbridge, Co Kilkenny, his father, Sgt. Michael Gleeson, was hoping that John F. Kennedy would win the United States Presidential election, and had arranged to sit up that night in a friend's house to hear the results on the radio.

At McKee Park, North Circular Road, Dublin, Mrs McGuinn was wondering when she should send the card she had bought for her son's 22nd birthday on December 19th, while at Clanronald Road, Donnycarney, Trooper Fennell's family had not decided what to send him for his 19th birthday on December 27th. It was much the same story at the homes of the other families of the ill-fated patrol. Unaware of the tragedy, families were going about their chores in the normal way.

That evening, Comdt. James Breen, the Army Press Officer, received a telephone call at his home in Dublin at 6.55—it would then have been about 8.55 in Katanga—from his friend Fr. James Stone in Killester. The common hobby of salmon angling on the River Liffey and elsewhere had cemented a great friendship between these two. Fr. Stone was also a keen amateur radio operator, and was now telling Breen that he had been in clear contact with the 32nd Battalion in Goma.

The link between Fr. Stone and the Irish troops in the Congo had begun in September. One morning during that month, Capt. Brendan Deegan, Athlone, signals officer of the 32nd, had tuned into the amateurs band (40 metre) of his C12 radio set and listened to some American missionaries chatting. Just to see if he could get the range with his C12, he decided to call one of them, using the Curragh amateur call sign EI5C, and was delighted when immediately answered. When told who he was speaking to, the missionary said he regularly spoke to an amateur in Jinja, Uganda, an Irishman by the name of Terry Tierney. He also arranged for Deegan to contact Tierney the following morning. Tierney, it transpired, was an old friend of Fr. Stone's. Before going to Jinja, to work at the big hydro-electric scheme there, he had been an engineer with the Electricity Supply Board, and he and Fr. Stone had often fished together. In Dublin, Tierney had collected as many pieces of wireless equipment as he thought he would need, should they not be available in Uganda, and of course, Fr. Stone was able to contribute to this reserve.

For approximately a month, Tierney served as a link between the troops at Goma and Fr. Stone in Dublin. Then Tierney made an extremely nice gesture to his peacekeeping compatriots. From the reserve parts he had brought with him from Ireland, including some of those Fr. Stone had given him, he built a transmitter which could get Ireland direct. Then he drove from Jinja to Kisoro on the Uganda-Congo border, a journey of more than 300 miles, and presented it to Deegan. Now the battalion could talk to Fr. Stone direct.

Knowing that the Chief of Staff, Maj. Gen. Sean Mac Eoin, had expressed a wish to talk to the battalion if it were possible, Fr. Stone rang Breen on the Tuesday night. "Jim," he said, "I have Goma on now perfect." He suggested Gen. Mac Eoin should talk to Goma the following morning, as the move of the 32nd to Kamina base was nearing completion. Accordingly arrangements were made for the Chief of Staff to be at Fr. Stone's house at 10.30 a.m. next day.

When the arrangement was made, the ambush had not yet been discovered, but at about nine o'clock on Wednesday morning as Comdt. Breen was leaving for the office, his telephone rang again. This time it was a reporter from a Dublin newspaper seeking confirmation of an earlier B.B.C. news bulletin that Irish soldiers had been killed at Niemba. Unable to confirm the report, Breen informed Col. Brendan Barry, Director of Intelligence, of it, and then took the liberty of telephoning the Chief of Staff at his home. The report, Breen informed the Chief of Staff, was rather hazy and did not state the number of soldiers involved or their names. Gen. Mac Eoin was inclined to disbelieve it, hoping that it was false or at least exaggerated. His appointment with Fr. Stone to talk to the 32nd Battalion now took on a new significance.

As Capt. Jack Millar of the Army Press Office had received a letter from Gleeson about his radio programmes, it was known who the officer in Niemba was. It was not known, of course, if he was among those reported killed, although mention had been made of an officer having been involved.

At 10.25 a.m. seated at the keyboard of the recently-installed Telex machine in the Congo Room of Army headquarters, Millar sent a query through the U.N. in the Congo asking if there was any truth in the report.

A short time later, the Chief of Staff and Breen arrived at Fr. Stone's house in Killester. Contact was made with Goma at 11.20 and Gen. Mac Eoin talked to Col. Buckley, the battalion commander. Having picked up Enright's radio messages, the 32nd had been following the grim news and so Buckley was in a position not only to give confirmation, but some details, including a full list of names of the missing patrol. This, of course, Buckley emphasised, was not an official list of those involved. Fr. Stone then wrote down the names—G as in Golf, L as in Lima, E as in Echo, E as in Echo, S as in Sierra, O as in Oscar, N as in November (Gleeson), K as in Kilo, E as in Echo, L as in Lima, L as in Lima, Y as in Yankee (Kelly), and so on.

The Chief of Staff telephoned the Minister for Defence, Kevin Boland, who had already been notified of the report, and passed the information on to him. Then, a short time later, at the Fianna Fail Ard-Fheis in the Mansion House, Dublin, the Taoiseach, Sean Lemass interrupted the normal business of the conference and announced the sad news.

"I regret to inform the Ard-Fheis," he said, "that a report has been received by the Minister for Defence that a patrol of Irish soldiers serving with the United Nations forces in Katanga Province of the Congo has been ambushed, and that some of them have been killed."

The Taoiseach went on to tell the shocked delegates: "Information is not yet precise as to the extent of the casualties. This is very distressing news indeed, and I am sure the Ard-Fheis will wish to record our sorrow that Irish lives should be lost, and that our deep sympathy be conveyed to the relatives of those who died."

The sad news shocked the nation almost to the point of disbelief. As *The Irish Times* reported: "By mid-day the news had spread, and many thousands of people throughout the country tuned in to the B.B.C. hourly news bulletins, and then to the 1.30 news on Radio Eireann for more details. There was also a big demand for the Dublin evening newspapers, which appeared on the streets earlier then usual with all available information.

"An atmosphere of shock and a general anxiety for more news of the incident prevailed in an unusually silent Dail in the afternoon, and not long after the House began the day's deliberations, Mr James Dillon, Leader of the Opposition, asked the Taoiseach if he would make a statement about the sad news emanating from the Congo."

Remarking that the members of the House, no doubt, had already heard the tragic news, Mr Lemass said that in spite of the efforts of the Minister for Defence to ascertain the full facts, the information available was not yet complete. However, he said, it appeared that an 11-man patrol operating from Niemba had been attacked. It had been reported that some bodies were seen at the scene of the attack. One member of the patrol had escaped with injuries and was believed to be in hospital.

"I know," the Taoiseach said, "that every member of Dail Eireann is profoundly grieved by the event. The men who have died have bravely given their lives in a most noble cause—the maintenance of peace." He added that strong forces had now been dispatched to recover the bodies, and to locate the missing members of the patrol.

At Army headquarters, the Telex machine chattered continuously throughout the day in an exchange of messages between Dublin and Leopoldville and Dublin and Elizabethville, that was to continue for several days almost non-stop. The Minister for Defence and the Chief of Staff were among those who anxiously scanned incoming messages for scraps of information that would give them some idea of what had happened.

What they were most anxious for was for U.N. confirmation of the names of members of the patrol so that they could be released and end an agonising wait for the families of hundreds of soldiers who by no stretch of the imagination could have been involved.

At approximately four o'clock on Wednesday afternoon, 10 names and serial numbers of members of the patrol still unaccounted for, finally came through. But again, 57 Private Thomas Kenny had been confused with 67 Trooper Thomas Kenny, and the wrong man was posted missing. The result was that the similarity in name and number which previously had caused minor misunderstandings, now caused a family needless heartache.

FIFTEEN

Baluba and Booby Traps

As the Taoiseach had informed the Dail, strong forces were converging on Niemba that morning. Rescue helicopters and spotter planes were being flown up from Kamina, Comdt. Hogan's patrol was driving towards Niemba from Albertville, though in a rainstorm which reduced the road to an appalling condition, and Comdt. Barry was leading a 45-man patrol northwards from Manono.

Barry's mission was to help in locating missing members of Gleeson's patrol as only four bodies had been seen. At Kiambi he spoke to the chief and others, who knew that the Baluba had been in action in the Niemba area, but had assumed that it had been against the gendarmerie. Near Kasempele, about 30 miles north of Kiambi, Barry's patrol was setting up a wireless station, when two large truckloads of armed Baluba—about 120 in all—approached from the south. Stopped and questioned, they stated that they were going to Niemba to join in the fighting. The troops told them that their information was that a Baluba party had ambushed an Irish-U.N. patrol. This they refused to believe.

Barry insisted, however, and further informed them that the fighting was over and that they should return to their homes. Col. Bunworth then instructed Barry to return to Manono and send a further strong patrol towards Niemba at first light the following morning.

Back in Manono, Comdt. Barry received a rather surprising offer. Mr. Shebani, the Manono representative in the Provincial Parliament, offered to send 100 Baluba towards Niemba next morning to help in the search for the missing members of the patrol. However, Barry, while he realised that a small party of pro-U.N. Baluba would be of great help, had to decline the offer as the presence of Baluba in the search area could lead to much confusion.

As it was, there were more than enough Baluba around Niemba, as Comdt. Hogan and his patrol discovered when they arrived at the bridge over the River Lukuga. Chief Kasanga-Niemba's warriors had sabotaged the 90-ft. long bridge by tearing up the planking for a distance of about 15 feet at both ends. At the same time, Enright informed them on the radio that over 100 warriors were massing at the railway station (a railway employee later put the number at 300).

The troops were deployed in defensive positions until Raftery and his men recovered the planking from the bed of the river and repaired the bridge. The patrol then advanced, the infantry in battle formation giving flank protection to the vehicles. Several native houses were searched on the way in, in case they might be harbouring Baluba gathering for an attack, but were found to be deserted, and the patrol entered Niemba at 3 p.m. Plans were now made to move on the railway station, and drive the Baluba out, but were not put into effect as a message was received from Col. Byrne stating: "(a) Act in accordance with U.N. directive—no reprisals; (b) recover bodies and identify."

By this time, an Ethiopian patrol had arrived from Nyunzu, and with Sergeant Michael Nolan who had come out with Enright, and Corporals Lynch and McGrath, was leaving for the ambush area. The Ethiopians had two Baluba prisoners, who tried to escape some distance down the Manono road by jumping out of the truck, but were recaptured. Lynch was taking no chances on this trip. He had six hand-grenades tucked inside his shirt.

Capt. Crowley followed with a patrol of 36 men, and joined the Ethiopians in the search at the bridge. Five bodies were recovered. Thirty yards from Gleeson, Gaynor, Dougan and McGuinn, Kelly had been found. In the gathering darkness, they were taken back to Niemba by the combined Irish-Ethiopian patrol. Two new roadblocks were encountered on the return journey, including a felled tree only a mile from Niemba.

In anticipation of an attack on the post, Comdt. Hogan had prepared a scheme of defence during the afternoon. Enright and von Beyer took a party to the Lukuga River and booby-trapped the bridge by placing grenades under the planks in such a manner that they would explode only if the planks were lifted. To cover the approaches to the houses at the crossroads, gun posts were set up in suitable positions, such as windows, rooftops and verandahs. Where necessary, holes were broken in the walls. Fields of fire were cleared, tripwires with tin cans attached were strung at the edge of the bush, which in some cases came right up to the backs of the houses, and vehicles so placed that their headlights could be used to illuminate the surrounding area in the event of a night attack.

During the night, the fires of the Baluba could be seen burning in the bush, but they did not attack, and next morning, having consulted a sketch prepared by Fitzpatrick, Comdt. Hogan and Capt. Crowley set off with a strong patrol of Irish and Ethiopian troops to search again for the missing members of Lt. Gleeson's patrol. Fitzpatrick had offered to return to the scene of the ambush and assist in the search, but it was felt that he had gone through enough, and that the remainder of the patrol would be found not far from the others.

SIXTEEN
Back from the Dead

A bird chirped in the scrub, and something stirred in the swamp below. Private Kenny found that he was still alive, and hearing the bird chirping above his head realised that the battle was over. For him, however, a long fight for survival was only beginning.

After his tormentors had charged over him towards the sound of Browne's shots, he was to report, he did not hear the Gustaf any more. There was silence for a while. "Some time later," he recalled, "I heard moans on my left. I couldn't move with pain. Then about half an hour later I heard a single rifle shot. I lay in the same spot for a long time. It became dark. I thought I smelt fire and the smell of burning flesh. I must have become delirious. I tried to get up in the darkness, but I wasn't able to rise off the ground until morning..."

At what time Kenny became conscious of the fact that the battle was over, must remain a matter of conjecture. Time, as he recalls, was gone. But as the bird was chirping over his head, he knew that the warriors had departed. His left hand was still over his face, and was hot and sticky. At first he was unable to pull it away, and when he did so, he saw that the murky swamp water beneath him was purple with his blood. He thought he would have a smoke and see where he was. He looked at his right hand. It was still out in front of him, bruised and badly swollen.

Kenny believed that he was going to die from the wounds very soon, and the thought persisted in his mind that he would have a smoke while waiting to die. He was lying half on his right side and with his left hand he took his cigarettes out of his left breast pocket and a box of safety matches from his left trouser pocket. He was unable to move his right hand or legs because of the great pain in them. The dye from the two Sabena Airways baggage labels which he had kept as souvenirs of his first travel abroad had gone into some photographs and around the packet of cigarettes, though the cigarettes themselves were dry. But the matches were wet and fell apart, and the blood from his lips and his sticky hand made the cigarettes wet also and he put the packet back in his pocket.

Hearing a crackle in the bushes and thinking that the warriors had come back to look for him, he froze back into his original position. He had a feeling that there were eyes watching him and he lay dead still for some time. Then he heard the shot. It was followed by a whistle, and he had the urge to call out. At the same time, he knew that if it was his own men they would whistle again. There was no further whistle, and he decided that the shot had been fired by his attackers with one of their new-found toys.

The next thing to plague his mind was the thought that he could smell smoke and burning flesh and hear the crackling of the fire coming nearer and nearer. He did not want to be burned to death after living so long, and thinking that he would rather get out and die in the bush if no one picked him up, he struggled to his feet. No sooner was he on his feet, however, than he tripped over a branch and fell. "Kenny," he said to himself, "you're finished." Somehow he got to his feet again, but he had forgotten his helmet, and fearing that the Baluba might find it and come looking for him again, he retrieved it. The he noticed blotches of rain on the large water leaves and thirstily licked them off. The thoughts of having a smoke were still with him, and it occurred to him that if he got out he could get a light from the fire. Soon, though, he realised that there was no fire. The crackling had just been the sound of the falling rain ...

As the night had passed a sense of time had returned to Kenny, and although half delirious he had been thinking how long it would take a rescue patrol to reach the bridge. He had no watch, but always had been good at telling the time without one. He estimated that it would take a patrol until 7 a.m. to arrive, and wondered what he was going to do if he found himself out in the bush about 4 or 5 a.m. as he would be visible to any warriors who might return to have another look for those who had escaped.

Now he found himself walking out of the swamp. "The two arrows were sticking in me and causing me great pain," he was to report. "My head was numb and the back of it was bleeding badly. There was blood in my eyes and I couldn't see very well. My hands and arms were swollen and very painful ..." He came across an upturned blue beret, Killeen's he was later told. There was a note or letter in it, but he could not lift the beret as he was holding his helmet in his left arm as his head was too sore to put in on, and his right hand was injured. Anyway, the patrol would find it. Then he saw the cars of a patrol coming far off in the distance. He estimated that it was about 5.a.m. It would take too long for the cars to reach him, he thought, and he did not know what was in the 300 yards of bush between himself and the bridge. Maybe the ambushers were still there, perhaps prowling around, or hiding in anthills. Perhaps they lived just down the road…

Determined not to let the Baluba get another chance to kill him, he decided to go round in a circle, away from the scene of the fight.

While walking through the bush, Kenny became delirious again. He saw a bridge leading across the river to a native house, but was afraid to go near it in case it might be occupied. He cut to the left along the river. Then he heard shots, rifle shots he thought, and feared the occupants of the house had seen him. The river looked too deep to cross. But one minute it was in front of him, then he found somehow that it was behind him. Yet he was not wet. Now he estimated that it was about noon. The sun was beating down upon him with a merciless heat, and he had to put a handkerchief on his head to shield himself from it. Then he saw a red plane, and took the handkerchief off his head and waved to it. But it went off. Perhaps if he could light a fire he could attract its attention. He took out the small square magnifying glass he had found in the trader's shop only the previous morning but now an eternity away, and tried to light a fire. But he could not get the grass to light.

In his subsequent wanderings, Kenny was in a state of delirium and experienced a nightmarish mixture of fact and fantasy. On the bank of the river he thought he met a soldier-carpenter from Albertville. A white plane passed over, but he was unable to attract its attention either. In fact, both a white plane and a red plane would have passed over the area. He remembers becoming hungry during the afternoon, seeing two young Congolese hiding behind a tree, asking them to bring food and waving 10 francs at them. They did not come over to him, and he felt very disappointed. Then, afraid that if they brought anyone they would kill him for the 10 francs he had in his pocket, he wandered away from them. He imagined

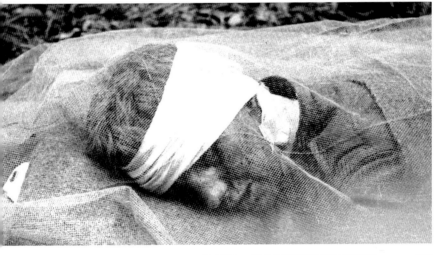

TOP LEFT: *Wounded and dazed, Kenny staggers from the bush 41 hours after the ambush. Acting Sgt. J. Reilly (left) and Dr. Brendan Heaney give a helping hand.*

TOP RIGHT: *Kenny smokes a cigarette while the arrows are removed in a roadside operation.*

CENTRE: *As he waits for the helicopter, Kenny rests beneath a mosquito net.*

RIGHT: *Kenny is put aboard a helicopter for evacuation from the ambush area.*

Liam Dougan

Anthony Browne

Michael McGuinn

Thomas Fennell

Joseph Fitzpatrick

Patrick ('Willie') Davis

Peter Kelly

Matty Farrell

Kenny with the battalion O/C Col. Bunworth at Albertville before going to Elizabethville to convalesce.

Pictured with the two survivors: Comdt. McMahon, Pte. Kenny, Pte. Fitzpatrick, Col. Bunworth, Lt. von Beyer and Comdt. Hogan.

the red plane landed in a field but was unable to take him. He thought he saw and talked to old friends, including Gleeson, Dougan, McGuinn and Kelly, who were then dead, and Dr. Heaney who had given him an injection at the Filtisaf factory before he left Albertville for Niemba.

All the time there was at the back of Kenny's mind the thought that Niemba was also under attack by the Baluba and that if he arrived there, members of the garrison would try and bring him in and perhaps get killed doing so.

It was his sub-conscious aim, therefore, to try to reach the railway line on either side of Niemba, so that he could stop a train and raise the alarm. However, he was not as near Niemba as his sub-conscious led him to believe. He spent a cold night rolling deliriously in the long grass, and on Thursday morning, after further wanderings in which he slaked his thirst with raindrops gathered in his helmet from the bullrushes, he followed the path which he thought he had seen the doctor take, and praying to the Blessed Virgin to guide him, he eventually found the road.

It was then that Comdt. Hogan's patrol was driving down the Manono road towards the scene of the ambush. At 7 a.m. the leading vehicle rounded a bend just beyond the village of Tundulu, on the left-hand side about 1½ miles from the bridge, and Capt. Crowley saw a Congolese walking towards him about 300 yards away. On seeing the vehicle, the man immediately dived into the bush. Realising that information from him might prove very valuable to them, Crowley fired two short bursts of his Gustaf over the position where he had taken cover. They slowed down the vehicle as they approached the spot, but the man had gone. The sound of the shots, however, had been heard by Kenny who immediately took cover on the left side of the road.

"I had travelled about half a mile further on," Crowley was to report, "and my vehicle was climbing out of a slight ravine when, along a drain on my left I saw a figure in U.N. shirt and slacks with his arms raised above his head. We raised a cheer for him as we went towards him as he looked quite dazed, very fatigued and was obviously overcome by the sight of us. As I reached him, he raised his right arm in the form of a salute and said: '57 Kenny Sir,' I congratulated him on his escape, and the two N.C.O.s with me did likewise. He kept repeating: 'God bless you lads.' "

Kenny, who had been hiding in a drain at a right-angle to the road, having thought that Baluba warriors were coming down the road, with captured guns, dragged himself to his feet when the patrol pulled up. He recalls: "I heard someone say 'Good old Kenny'. I saw this man and he said: 'Who are you?' and I said I was '57 Kenny, reporting.' He paused for a second, looking at me and I said: 'You are Comdt. P.D. Hogan . . .' "

"He was in a bad way," Hogan later reported. "But he was able to stand up straight and tell me his name when I asked him. His head was badly battered, and his hair was matted with blood. His right hand was also badly battered and swollen. His legs were cut and torn, he had an arrow wound in his neck and two barbed arrows were hanging from his rump. He had been wandering wounded in the bush since the ambush 41 hours before."

Comdt. Heaney whom Kenny imagined had spoken to him in his wanderings in the bush, now really did come to his aid, and with the help of Cpl. Roche, also of the Army Medical Corps, and an Ethiopian medical orderly, the arrows were removed, and the wounds treated and bandaged. During the roadside operation, Kenny smoked a cigarette a soldier had given him, and tried to warn the patrol of the danger uppermost in his mind—the anthills which some of the warriors had used as camouflage. "Mind the anthills," he kept saying, "Mind the anthills."

A corporal informed him that another member of the patrol also had made it to safety, and he asked if it had been McGuinn, who had been closer to him than any of the others, but was told it was not.

Comdt. Hogan notified Col. Bunworth by radio that a second survivor had been found, and arrangements were made to evacuate Kenny by helicopter from a village clearing north of their position. The helicopter landed at 10 a.m., and Dr. Burke who came in it, joined the patrol, while Dr. Heaney flew back with the injured soldier to Niemba.

The patrol then went on to the bridge to continue the search for the four missing members of Gleeson's patrol.

With the help of the tracking skill of the Ethiopians, the bodies of Farrell, Killeen and Fennell were found about 300 yards westward along the river bank. Nearby were two newly-dug graves containing at least one Baluba each.

Now only one member of the patrol was missing—Trooper Browne. Wide areas on both sides of the road were searched and searched again. Overhead, observers in a spotter plane and a helicopter scanned the bush. Capt. Sloane dropped a message from the plane informing the patrol that a lorry load of Baluba had been sighted about two miles south, heading for the bridge, and had scattered when the plane swooped low over them. Of Browne, however, there was no sign. Every search party which returned to the bridge reported negative.

Although the searchers could not know, it would be two long years before the bush would yield the secret of Browne's fate.

SEVENTEEN

The Prisoner of Kiambi

As Comdt. Hogan's patrol had been setting out from Niemba, a patrol of 30 Irish and 15 Moroccans had been leaving Manono under Capt. Patrick Condron, with instructions to go north towards Niemba, intercept any prisoners who might have been taken by the Baluba and locate the two missing vehicles. The patrol was to spend the night in Kiambi and link up with a patrol from Niemba next day, Friday.

As the patrol was about to leave the post, a lorry and bus containing about 100 armed Baluba pulled up at the gate, a small warrior wearing a leopard skin marched over to Condron in military fashion, saluted, and informed him that on the instructions of Mr Shebani they were placing themselves under his command and would help in every way possible. Not wishing to arrive at the ambush scene with 100 Baluba, Condron began to argue his way out of it, and then came a heaven-sent reprieve—a tyre on the bus went flat. Condron was delighted, told them to follow on, and moved off with his patrol.

About 13 miles out of Manono the patrol stopped a lorry which was found to contain 10 Baluba who had been shot and wounded in the ambush. Questioned through an interpreter they denied that any U.N. troops had been involved in the ambush, but said it was a gendarmerie patrol which had attacked them. Asked what colour were the soldiers' helmets, they admitted they were blue. Pointing to Condron's helmet, however, one of them said that they did not have the letters "U.N." in front of the helmets. This may have been true in some cases as the U.N. operation was still in a fairly early stage, but the argument is hardly significant since Kasanga-Niemba's parting instruction subsequently quoted in court specifically mentioned the Irish.

The wounded denied that they had taken any soldiers prisoner, adding that the only prisoner they had taken was a Conakat whom they had left in the jail in Kiambi. The only weapon uncovered in a search of the lorry was a bow and arrow under the driver's seat. The wounded, who were being driven by natives of Kiambi to the hospital in Manono, were allowed to proceed, and Condron notified Comdt. Barry to expect them.

In the hope of getting further information from the Congolese prisoner whom the wounded claimed to have been with Gleeson's patrol, Condron continued to Kiambi, crossed the river and set off in search of the jail. However he took a wrong turn and came to a small infirmary which had been part of a Belgian administrative post about 500 yards from the village proper.

There he saw the missing Landrover on one side of the infirmary and the Volkswagen pick-up on the other side. He and his men immediately surrounded the building and rushed in.

A native medical orderly whom they surprised in the main room told them there was a body in a small adjoining room. There on a table under a white sheet the troops found the body of a Congolese. He was wearing white pants and white shirt, and had a blood-stained pad on his stomach. He had been killed by a bullet which had gone right through him.

Condron asked the medical orderly where the two vehicles had come from, but he said he did not know. On inspection it was found that there were five bullet holes on the left, or driver's door of the pick-up, the bullet's having ripped out through the name of M. Amarshi Fils. Whether this burst was fired by Gleeson's patrol in the engagement on the roadside, or by a warrior accidentally discharging a captured gun afterwards, is not clear.

When the troops were examining the vehicles the medical orderly fled. Unable to take the vehicles with them, the patrol removed the tops of the distributors so that they could not be started and driven away.

With the full patrol now across the river, Condron, convinced that the dead man was not the prisoner mentioned by the wounded, moved up to the village jail. The jailer, a local man, said that the prisoner had been taken outside the village to work, but was evasive when asked where exactly he was then. All the prisoners in the jail also were interrogated, but gave no additional information, and no trace of the man alleged to have been taken prisoner from Gleeson's patrol was ever found. According to

Kenny they neither had a Congolese guide nor had given anyone a lift.

On arrival at the main council hut in the centre of the village, Condron and his troops received a very cool reception. The villagers, fearing that the U.N. was there for revenge, were ready for trouble.

All the menfolk were armed with bows and arrows, and many of them had taken up positions behind trees and at the sides of houses. The chief refused to talk to Condron in front of the patrol, but agreed to do so behind the hut, and there Condron discussed the situation with him. In an argument about the cars, Condron accused the chief of being involved in the ambush, but the old man maintained that the vehicles had arrived there the night before with the wounded, and that his people had nothing to do with it. He also said that he was going to keep the vehicles, presumably because he had given the wounded a truck in exchange for them. Condron, however, informed him that he could not do so as they were U.N. property.

As the patrol was about to leave Kiambi and push north, Shebani's contingent of Baluba arrived at the ferry and wanted to go along, the one in the leopard skin informing Condron that he was ready for duty. This time Condron suggested that they would be better employed guarding Kiambi just in case the gendarmerie had been involved in the ambush, while the patrol went ahead to investigate. The little man in the leopard skin was delighted to get something to do, so the patrol continued towards Niemba alone.

The farther north the troops went the cooler the reception they got. On arrival at Kabeke, about 60 miles north of Kiambi, it was found that the patrol's radio was out of action, and one of the trucks had a bad oil leak from the sump. As it was then 3.30 p.m., Condron decided to return to Kiambi for the night. There the set was repaired, and in contact with headquarters once more, the patrol was ordered to return to Manono if possible as an overnight stay in Kiambi was now considered undesirable. At this stage the people of Kiambi were anxious for the patrol to stay as they were not quite sure what had happened in Niemba and wanted protection. At the same time they were reluctant to provide the ferry service during darkness.

Condron, however, succeeded in persuading the chief to make the ferry available and taking Gleeson's vehicles, returned to Manono, leaving

Shebani's contingent of warriors to continue their job of "protecting" Kiambi. The engine of one of one of the recovered vehicles, it was found, had seized, and had to be towed all the way back to Manono. A fitter on the patrol succeeded in starting the other and it was driven back. Later the people of Kiambi, realising that they could not have the trucks, handed over the keys to the U.N. in Manono.

EIGHTEEN

Night Alert

When Hogan's and Condron's patrols were on the outward journey from Niemba and Manono, Col.Byrne and Comdt. O'Brien were flying towards Niemba by helicopter from Albertville.

Comdt. McMahon, who was left in charge of the post, had the defences moved more into the open to provide better observation of the approaches to the garrison in the daylight. A patrol under Lt. Enright was sent to the bridge over the River Lukuga to remove the grenades and collect water. The bridge had not been interfered with during the night. The warriors had now gone from the railway station, but presumably were still somewhere in the surrounding bush. With the departure of Comdt. Hogan's patrol, tension increased in the garrison, and in order to boost morale and let it be known to whatever tribal forces were in the area that they would get a powerful rebuff if they attacked, McMahon ordered the firing of an anti-tank grenade into the valley between the post and a nearby village.

About this time a signal was received notifying McMahon that Col. Byrne would be expected at 9 a.m., and trees were cleared to provide a landing area for this and other helicopters, which would be evacuating dead and wounded. As soon as Col. Byrne and Comdt. O'Brien landed, the helicopter took off again to pick up Kenny who had been found by Hogan's patrol.

Col. Byrne then examined the defensive positions and expressed satisfaction with the general plan, which was to pull in the defences and defend from the houses in the event of an attack.

Just after Comdt. Heaney landed in Niemba with Kenny to pick up Fitzpatrick, one of the sentries on the rooftops raised the alarm that the Baluba were coming, and firing began. Like the helicopter crew and everyone else in the open, Pte. J.J. Shields of Tralee, who had been peeling potatoes outside the "Guest House" grabbed his gun and ran for cover. As the firing stopped, however, Shields was wounded in the abdomen by a ricocheting bullet accidentally discharged. Fortunately the wounds were not fatal, and he was evacuated with Kenny and Fitzpatrick to Albertville, where they were met by another battalion doctor, Comdt. Brendan Boylan, and taken to hospital.

In Niemba, a tense silence returned, as sentries scanned the impenetrable bush in expectation of a Baluba attack. If the sentries felt that there were eyes watching them from the bush, they were not mistaken. Every move made at Niemba was being watched, as was shown by a report on conversations that were made on the railway telephone that day and intercepted at Albertville. The system was of the type that simply by lifting a telephone, persons at different points could listen in or converse, and while the report does not help to clarify the organisational set-up behind the ambush, it is worth recording.

The conversations were between persons in Nyunzu, Kilima a few miles west of Niemba, and in Niemba itself, presumably in the station area, about half a mile from the U.N. post. The first was made at 7.30 a.m., and was recorded by the interceptor as follows: "Nyunzu asks Kilima how this story with the U.N. will terminate. Answer: One should have thought of that before killing people." The next one was at 8.30 a.m., and read: "Nyunzu instructs the whole line of communications to transmit the following to the cartel:

"1, remove caps made of animal skins; 2, henceforth not to move in groups ; 3, hide their 'poisons' and arms in their houses; 4, wait until the enemy is quite close before fetching their 'poisons', caps and arms to proceed with the attack." This, Nyunzu added, was an order "from the president of the cartel and Chief Mulongo on instructions from the Ethiopians." The latter remark presumably was a garbled reference to an order by the Ethiopian-U.N. garrison in Nyunzu, forbidding Baluba to move in armed groups following the ambush.

Four further conversations monitored that day were as follows: "9.15 a.m. Nyunzu states that people of the cartel shall henceforth not walk in groups to the 'halts' (this could mean roadblocks or stopping points). One man at a time only, if necessary. 9.55. Niemba says to Nyunzu: I hear shots fired by the Irish. 10.00. Niemba says that a man from the cartel went to see the number of people killed on the side of the cartel during their engagement with the U.N. According to what he had seen there were six killed and seven wounded. 15.00. Niemba states that since this morning five helicopters have landed at Niemba."

With Kenny rescued, the mistake in identities was discovered. Mr. and Mrs. Kenny, Balinteer Cottages, Dundrum, Dublin, were given the happy news that their son had not been in the ambush, while Mrs. Rose Kenny, North King Street, Dublin, was informed that her husband had been in the ambush but happily, had survived.

Reports on the survivors' condition were now coming up on the Telex in Army headquarters in Dublin, and the medical report on Kenny's condition just after he was found concluded with the following observation: "SEVERE DEHYDRATION AND EXHAUSTION AFTER 40 HRS. WITHOUT FOOD DRINK OR ATTENTION TO INJURIES STP MORALE VERY HIGH WHEN FOUND: MENTALLY ALERT, COOL, SELF-CONTROL PERFECT STP NO SELF-PITY STP SENSE OF DISCIPLINE AT ALL TIME PARADE GROUND, STEADY STP"

While two Dublin families got good news that day, there was still heartache in store for another. Fate had yet to deliver its final, cruel blow to the peacemakers of Niemba.

With the last of the bodies flown out to Albertville, Comdt. Hogan and Comdt. McMahon, assisted by other officers and Coy. Sgt. Keane, again organised the defence of Niemba for the night. As Hogan later reported of Keane, whom he had specially asked to accompany him to Niemba: "That night and the night before he was invaluable. His energy was tireless; he hardly slept at all; he was at hand at all hours of the night visiting the defence posts and encouraging the men. His selfless devotion to duty during the period considerably lightened the task of Comdt. McMahon and myself and deserves the highest commendation."

Much the same could be said of many of the others. Although the massacre of their comrades had left an indelible mark on their minds and continuous patrols, sentry duty and an expectation of a Baluba attack left them little time for sleep, the troops were comporting themselves in a manner which would have made their dead platoon commander proud.

Reporting on the events of the night, Comdt. Burke was to recall: "All this time a night attack had been expected, and everyone in the garrison at Niemba was alert and tense awaiting this attack."

Trouble came at 9 p.m., but not in the form expected. Sentries on a rooftop had been following, with the aid of a torch, the movement of branches which suggested someone was running from bush to bush. On glimpsing finally, what appeared to be the white shirt of a Baluba scout, and convinced that if the warrior got away with information on the garrison's guard positions, or even if he got the idea that the garrison would hesitate to shoot, a Baluba attack would follow at dawn, one of the sentries shouted a challenge. There was no response, and the sentry opened fire. Other sentries followed suit. A stray bullet severed the cable from the generator, cutting the power supply. Men who had been sleeping, exhausted on the floor, were galvanised into action.

On the verandah at the back of Gleeson's bungalow, Cpl. McGrath, Pte. Davis and Pte. Noel Byrne manning a Bren gun, waited expectantly. But the shooting soon subsided. Davis pulled back the Bren gun to unload. In the room behind, the young soldier who, scarcely a fortnight earlier had accidentally wounded Matafali, was awakened by the firing and reached for his sub-machine gun. Weary from long hours of patrolling and sentry duty, he was startled by a noise and the sight of a shadowy figure kneeling outside the French window. Thinking they were being attacked, he fired. Outside Pte. "Willie" Davis fell forward into the arms of Cpl. McGrath, mortally wounded. McGrath shouted for the doctor, and said an Act of Contrition into Davis's ear. Donnelly, who also had been sleeping in the room from which Davis had been shot, was by his friend's side almost immediately.

On examining Davis by torchlight, Dr. Burke realised that the only chance of saving him was to get him to hospital. At the same time he put Davis's chance of survival at less than one in a hundred. Donnelly asked for permission to accompany his friend, and the request was granted. Quickly Davis was placed on an air mattress in the back of one of the better sprung pick-up trucks, which left for Albertville with an escort under Lt. Raftery. Lt. Enright and another escort went with them to the Lukuga River to assist and help protect them in case the bridge had been damaged again. They found that the bridge, which had not been booby-trapped that night, had been interfered with by the Baluba once more. But engineer Raftery and his men quickly repaired it.

As the injured man was borne towards Albertville, battalion headquarters was asked to have an escorted ambulance meet him half way. However, two hours after leaving Niemba, Davis died, despite all that Burke and the medical orderlies travelling with him could do. Fr. Crowley, who had come out from Albertville in the ambulance, administered the last rights. The "Terrible Twins" were separated at last, though this time it was the one thing which no one wanted. And now Davis's secret would finally come out. Those who knew him as "Willie" would yet discover who he really was—Patrick Hubert Davis, a young man who had borrowed his dead brother's name so that he could be a soldier.

Here it is interesting to note that with regard to the initial firing from the rooftop, Comdt. Hogan later reported: "I formed the opinion that it was unlikely that there was an attack on the post imminent at the time. Nevertheless, in view of the dangerous situation, I did not think, and I do not think now, that the men were wrong in opening fire on the movement which they observed. They were convinced that they saw white-shirted figures in the bush and they fired only after shouting in the direction of the figures."

Col. Byrne, meanwhile, had decided that Niemba should be evacuated. Before reinforcements had been brought into Niemba, his forces had been, of necessity, already very thinly spread out, guarding many places and installations of much greater importance than Niemba. In fact, as he noted a short time after the ambush: "An examination of the map shows that at the time of writing, the U.N. has a total of 1,500 troops deployed over an area of North Katanga as large as England and Wales." To continue to garrison Niemba would have called for a much bigger force than originally stationed there, as it was now a very hostile area. Col. Byrne felt that Niemba did not warrant the use of so many men, and that they could be more usefully deployed elsewhere.

Another factor was that the accommodation and facilities that would be needed for the force which would now be required to garrison Niemba were just not available. As for Trooper Browne, the missing member of the patrol, all efforts to locate his body had failed. Col. Byrne, therefore, ordered Niemba to be evacuated on Friday, November 11th.

At noon on that day, the troops lined up, and in the course of a short address to them, Comdt. Hogan asked them to remember Lt. Gleeson and his comrades in their prayers. Then, at exactly five minutes past noon, the large blue and white United Nations flag which Lt. Gleeson had raised over Niemba only five weeks before, was taken down, and the people who had so cruelly rejected the help so generously given by Gleeson and his men were left so much the poorer.

NINETEEN

A Secret Order

Col. Byrne had intended flying to Dublin to make a personal report on the ambush but because of the local situation and the fact that the Chief of Staff, and the Quartermaster General, Col. Sean Collins-Powell had already arranged to make a tour of inspection of the Irish troops in the Congo early in December, he did not go.

Instead, in Albertville the weekend after the ambush, a tape recording of the accounts of several of those involved in the operation, including Fitzpatrick, was made and flown to Dublin, where it was played over to the President, Mr. de Valera, the Taoiseach, Mr. Lemass, the Minister for Defence and Chief of Staff. On this tape, Col. Bunworth said of Lt. Gleeson: "He had many difficulties to overcome, particularly those of accommodation. However, he overcame these difficulties and indeed his post was a model. It was spic and span . . . I considered this one of my best and most active outposts, in which the leadership of Lt. Gleeson and the enthusiasm of the other ranks was much admired throughout the battalion."

Col. Byrne, who also contributed to the tape, mentioned that he had given definite instructions to one political representative "to waste no time in finding out for me the reasons for this affair . . ." This was Mr. Shebani in Manono.

Mr. Shebani, strange as it may seem, arranged to have Mass sung in Manono by the local people the following Monday for the U.N. soldiers killed in the ambush. Yet, when he later submitted in writing, answers to questions which Col. Byrne put to him on Friday, November 11th, the best he could do was to accuse the Irish troops of opening fire first. The questions and answers are as follows:

Q. Why did the Baluba attack the U.N. Irish patrol?

A. Populations of Niemba attacked U.N. because the soldiers came with brutal intentions to the place where the Baluba had cut the road and blown up the bridge. After a short discussion between the soldiers and Baluba, the U.N., without hesitation, began to fire on the Baluba, and immediately there were three killed among the Baluba. In order to defend themselves, the Baluba then fired on the soldiers and killed approx. nine of them. The population of Niemba accuses and condemns the reprehensible actions of the U.N. Thus, the population of Niemba criticises the work the U.N. troops are doing in Albertville.

Q. What action has been taken by Mr. Shebani or anybody else to punish those responsible?

A. The measures to be taken in that region need aim at maintaining peace and order which is the normal U.N. mission here in the Congo. One must help this people (of the Baluba) who do not understand the tasks of the U.N. here. In order to make that population understand, a population presently without any political leader from our political party, the Balubakat, I prefer to arrange a meeting here in Manono, of all the tribal chiefs of the Territory of Nyunzu, especially those of Niemba, together with the U.N. officers of Albertville and Nyunzu. As a representative of the Congolese people, I don't want the Congolese people to be killed by the U.N. soldiers, even if greater difficulties are encountered, for the U.N. forces must always hold the position of father of the family.

So much for Mr. Shebani. Soon he was expressing very different sentiments about the Irish-U.N. troops.

What about Mr. Jason Sendwé? He was quoted in the newspapers as claiming that the Baluba had mistaken the Irish for Belgians. "They do not know what the United Nations is," he was reported as saying. "They do not understand that the U.N. forces are there for their own protection. They hate all white men because they have seen the white men with Tshombé's gendarmerie. They do not understand the difference between those who lead the gendarmerie and those who serve the United Nations. That is why they attacked the Irish patrol. They set up a roadblock and attacked the first armed white men that came along. It was a tragic misunderstanding. We have no quarrel with the U.N."

It was to be shown that the Baluba of Niemba knew exactly who they were attacking. At the same time, Sendwé was probably correct in so far as the Baluba hatred of Europeans may have been a contributing factor. Gleeson and his men had encountered ample evidence of this anti-White feeling during their perilous visits to Nyunzu. Col. Byrne also had certain views on this point. He noted a short time after the ambush: "The events of Tuesday, November 8th at Niemba leave little doubt that North Katanga refuses to accept the European. My original plan, which had already been notified to Leopoldville, to replace the Mali battalion in North Katanga by troops of both 32nd and 33rd Irish battalions were cancelled by me because of that conviction. In an area where the white skin is anathema to the Balubakat warrior, it has been difficult to depend upon the Blue Helmet and U.N. goodwill as a means of protection. The Irish troops who lost their lives at Niemba had been there for a period of five weeks. They were known in the area because of their active patrolling. There were no gendarmerie nearer than Albertville. Any suggestion that they were mistaken for gendarmerie or that they were believed to be gendarmerie in disguise is sheer nonsense. Our patrols had been constantly on the Niemba-Kiambi road but it is significant that no attack was made on them until they appeared in small numbers.

Col. Byrne noted that one of the speakers on the telephone calls which had been intercepted, referred to the "Irish", and added: "He apparently was in no doubt as to their identity."

In Dublin, as a State funeral was being arranged for the victims of the ambush, messages were still being received from all over the world expressing shock that such an attack should have been made on members of a United Nations peace force. Representative of these was a message to Mr. Lemass from the Canadian Prime Minister, Mr. Diefenbaker, who stated: "I am shocked and distressed to learn of the brutal attack on a number of Irish soldiers serving with the United Nations in the Congo. Those who were killed have made a supreme sacrifice in fulfilment of an essential international duty in the cause of peace."

Mr. Kasavubu, President of the Congo, sent a cable to Mr. de Valera expressing "extreme regret at the death of Irish soldiers of the United Nations forces in north Katanga," and conveying his condolences to the families of the men. Mr. Tshombé expressed himself in similar terms. A message received on the Telex at Army headquarters in Dublin from the Congo read:

"PRESIDENT TSHOMBE HAS SENT A MESSAGE TO MR. BERENDSEN THE U.N. REPRESENTATIVE EXPRESSING HIS DEEP EMOTION AT LEARNING

THAT A DETACHMENT OF IRISH SOLDIERS HAD BEEN KILLED IN THE ALBERTVILLE DISTRICT AND ASKED THAT THE CONDOLENCES OF THE KATANGESE PEOPLE SHOULD BE EXTENDED TO THE FAMILIES."

While the tragedy might have been expected to sour the minds of the Irish public on the idea of an international peace force, the contrary proved to be the case, as was reflected in the leading articles in the national newspapers.

The Irish Times, which launched a most successful relief fund that was later to supplement Government provision for the dependents of the victims, commented that "these volunteers of Ireland died honourably, as honourably as any of the thousands of Irishmen who have given their blood in the services of other countries; more honourably perhaps since they shed it on behalf of the first genuine effort towards the policing of the world by an extra-national organisation."

The leading article also stated: "There is little likelihood that this horrible incident will affect the feeling of the Irish people otherwise than to sway it in the direction of an even more fervent loyalty to the doctrine of international peace and orderliness."

"If," it continued, "a third battalion of Irish troops is called for, the odds are that the response will be more enthusiastic than was the response for the first two." Ireland, it said, took pride in its membership of the United Nations, and was ready to face its obligations to the Charter, and added: "The new Bill to authorise the despatch of contingents to the U.N. forces which was on the Order Paper of Dail Eireann yesterday (Nov. 9th) will receive heartier support than ever."

"Through the tangle of complex motives and events, one fact shines clear," stated the *Irish Press*, "our men laid down their lives for peace and for a new world order.

"As the nation mourns, let it recall that the decision to co-operate was not taken lightly. It was taken in the full knowledge that this was a task we must accept if we were to remain faithful to the principles of justice and liberty by which we have always been guided.

"Our determination will not be shaken. Down the centuries men have died for justice and independence. As a nation, we could have no thought of betraying the trust of the past and the hope of the future. All will share the sorrow; all must be prepared to accept the sacrifice."

The *Irish Independent* stated: "In a Congo jungle yesterday, a number of Irish soldiers gave their lives on a mission of peace. When our troops set out last summer, we had all hoped that they would return unharmed and without memories of bloodshed. Yesterday's sad news has foiled that hope. But while the nation will lament with the relatives of these brave dead, it will also hold ever in honour the first of our National Army to give their lives on service abroad."

Later, when more details of Pte. Kenny's survival had got back to Dublin, the *Sunday Review*, then published by The Irish Times Ltd., referring to Kenny's composure when found, declared: "What superb discipline! What bravery!" and it went on: "Today, Ireland mourns, but today it can glory too, in the quality of its soldiers—soldiers like Pte. Kenny—and be proud of officers like the late Lt. Kevin Gleeson who walked through hostile Balubas to rescue single-handed, a Belgian priest."

But even in the midst of death there was life. Before the Telex machine at Army headquarters in Dublin was to become silent, the following message was to be sent, although Niemba had then been evacuated: "INFO FOR PTE DESMOND KEARNS NIEMBA YOUNG SISTER VANESSA BORN YESTERDAY."

With the arrival home to Ireland of the bodies of the Niemba dead and a State funeral in Dublin that evoked one of the greatest expressions of public sorrow ever experienced in the country, the story was ended so far as the world outside the Congo was concerned. Yet several important chapters had yet to be written, and the first of these was already begun.

When "B" Company of the 33rd Battalion was being flown from Manono to Albertville, a message in Irish which had been received from battalion headquarters was handed to Comdt. Beckett, the company doctor.

The message read: "FAN SA FEAR-O-NI-hEADH GORT AITHE A BHAILIU." Translated, it meant: "Stay in Manono to collect wounded."

TWENTY

Operation Shamrock

M r. Shebani had made it clear in his reply to Col. Byrne that the perpetrators of the ambush were not going to be punished by their own people, and the Katangese forces were not in a position to bring them to justice. The responsibility, therefore, fell on the section of the U.N. force directly involved.

The Irish patrol from Manono which had met the 10 injured Baluba, could, of course, have arrested them there and then and handed them over to the Katangese authorities, and that would not have been considered unreasonable, as feelings were naturally running high at that stage. However, the Irish, showing commendable restraint, allowed the ambushers to proceed to the Baluba hospital in Manono.

The question then arose as to what course of action should be taken when the 10 recovered. Were they to be allowed to fade into the bush, to resume their murderous activities, a living example to their fellow-tribesmen that law and order in the area had ceased to exist despite the presence of the U.N.? Apart from other disorders, such a course might well have been expected to encourage the belief that the U.N. forces could be attacked without fear of retribution.

Shortly after the ambush the matter was discussed in general terms by Col. Byrne and Col. Bunworth. Subsequently, its was considered by Col. Bunworth and his senior staff at a conference in the 33rd Battalion headquarters in Albertville, and it was agreed that an effort would be made to bring the 10 to account as soon as they were well. An examination of the position showed that to get them out of such a Baluba stronghold would be a difficult undertaking, fraught with many dangers. The fact that "B" Company was being transferred to Albertville as it was being replaced in Manono by Nigerian troops, would not make the operation any easier. Permission to plan and execute the proposed operation at a suitable date was sought from Col. Byrne in Elizabethville, and this, together with a promise to provide an aircraft at the appointed time, was readily given. Accordingly, the message to Dr. Beckett instructing him to remain in Manono, was the first step in a plan that was given the code name: "Operation Shamrock".

With the arrival of the 10 Baluba from Niemba, the number in the hospital at Manono rose to 134. Their arrival created a strong anti-Irish feeling in the hospital, and for some days afterwards, Dr. Beckett was forced to stay away from it. However, on the following Monday, he was able to return to the hospital, and although the Baluba had heavily reinforced their armed guard on the entrance gate and guards accompanied him on his round, he experienced no trouble. The 10, whose beds he found were also guarded, were mostly suffering from leg wounds. This showed that even when Gleeson and his men did open fire, they did not fire to kill, and though they probably did not know it, this was the best thing they could have done for their own protection, since a bullet could pass right through the chest of a crazed Baluba and not halt his deadly thrust, whereas a leg wound would put him out of action immediately.

Dr. Beckett ostensibly paid no more attention to the 10 from Niemba than any of the other injured. By this time three more Baluba had been admitted after another skirmish with the gendarmerie, bringing the total to 137. No other Irish visited the hospital, and thus no reason was given to lead the Baluba to suspect that any undue interest was being displayed in the warriors from Niemba. Any suspicions which may have existed were dispelled by the fact that the Irish were leaving. At that stage the Baluba were more concerned with the Nigerians who were having several skirmishes with them on a trek from Kamina which Col. Byrne noted "is surely becoming an epic."

Mr. Shebani now began to change his tune and whereas in his reply to Col. Byrne he was accusing the Irish of opening fire first on the Baluba, he addressed the following telegram to "Secretary General, United Nations, Leopoldville", on Nov. 20th.

"Balubakat population of Manono strongly protests against the departure of Irish and Moroccan troops. We have complete confidence in the Moroccans and Irish. Population demonstrate against the ONU manoeuvre. We preferred them to the Nigerians." In fact the Moroccan troops remained in Manono until relieved in December.

The precaution had been taken not long after the ambushers had been admitted, of marking the back of their bed cards with a small red ink cross on the top left corner, for identification purposes. But it was not until the last plane was ready to leave that Comdt. Beckett received the order to stay on to detain them. He was getting ready to board, in fact, when Capt. Condron handed him the message. The result was that the others taxied off, throwing their cigarettes to him as they went, and he was left. However, he was not alone. Cpl. Hoyne, Gleeson's signaller, had been flown down to Manono to help the Nigerians with their communications. He was also to be very helpful in "Operation Shamrock".

So far as the Baluba were concerned, Beckett was staying on in Manono as the Nigerians—the 4th Queens Own Nigerian Rifles—had no doctor with their advance party. Under "Operation Shamrock", however, his task was to forward periodic reports in Irish, through Hoyne, on the medical progress of the wounded Baluba in Niemba. This Beckett continued to do until the end of November.

In the meantime, pending a signal from Dr. Beckett that the warriors were ready to leave the hospital, the composition of the party whose mission it would be to take the Baluba from the Manono stronghold, was decided on a volunteer basis, its strength being dictated by the total number that would have to be brought back in the DC3 aircraft which they had been promised.

Once the decision had been made to carry out the operation, Comdt. Barry suggested that his company should take on the mission as it knew the area. Thus it was agreed that men of "B" Company would form the bulk of the party, Barry would command it, and on his request, battalion headquarters and "A" Company, of which the victims of the ambush had been members, also would be represented on it.

Comdt. Quigley, who had been in hospital with a leg ailment, was selected to represent battalion headquarters, and became operations officer on the mission at Barry's request. The other members selected were: Comdt. Louis Hogan, commander of "A" Company and the following men from "B" Company—

Captain Condron, Sgt M. Ryan, Sgt. W. Maher, Corporals M. Roche, E. Fox, W. Blake, T. Cunningham, and Troopers J.J. O'Connor and J. Harris—together with Lt. Roland Lindholm, "B" Company's Swedish interpreter. The men from "B" Company included three drivers who knew the terrain very well.

In Manono, Comdt. Beckett was going about his duties in the normal way, and had the odd drink with Shebani. Secretly, however, he had made certain arrangements with the Nigerian and Moroccan troops, as, in the absence of information from headquarters, he assumed that he was to go ahead with the planning of the operation.

On Nov. 30th, Comdt. Beckett decided that the Niemba Baluba were ready to leave, and sent the following message to battalion headquarters: "TA NA hEIN ULLAMH AN NEAD A FHAGAINT", informing Col. Bunworth that "the birds are ready to leave the nest." As subsequent events showed, he sent the message none too soon.

Since there was no way of identifying the Baluba once they were discharged, the Irish realised that they would have to move quickly. Consequently, "Operation Shamrock" was scheduled for first light on December 2nd, and a message was sent to Col. Byrne requesting the aircraft.

Later on Nov. 30th Col Byrne and Col. Bunworth discussed the operation by radio. The conversation was partly in Irish and partly in English for security reasons, and transmitted in Morse Code. Byrne began by asking if all or only some of the Baluba were ready, to which Bunworth replied that he was informed that all were ready.

The conversation went on: MUNA BHFUIL SIAD I SEOMRA AMHAIN (If they are not in one room) DO YOU ANTICIPATE A PROBLEM? *

WE ARE IN TOUCH WITH OUR DOCTIUR WHO IS RESPONSIBLE FOR AITNIU (recognition). PLAN ALLOWS FOR PRE-OP DISCUSSIONS BETWEEN HIM AND OIFIGEACH IC (officer in charge) OP. IF NOT AT ALL I SEOMRA AMHAIN (in one room) TASK WILL BE MORE DIFFICULT.

QONR (Queens Own Nigerian Rifles) MUST BE FULLY IN PICTURE. HAVE YOU A PLAN TO TAKE AR DOCTUIR AMAC NUAR A BHID SHIBH AG IMEACHT? (our doctor out when you will be leaving?)

ALPHA. MAJ. HOUGHTON FULLY BRIEFED BEFORE HE LEFT HERE 29TH

---

*The Publishers are aware that the spelling and use of Irish words leaves something to be desired. The messages are reproduced as they were sent.

NOV. FOR KAMINA. HE PROMISED FULL SUPPORT. WE SENT MESSAGE TO HAUGHTON TODAY ASKING FOR CONFIRMATION BRIGADIER APPROVAL AND COOP. NO REPLY YET. BRAVO. OUR DOCTUIR WILL BE EVAC NUAR OP CRIOCNUIGTE WITH AR PARTY (with our party when operation is finished).

PERSONS AG DEANAMH AN GABHAIL SAN OISPIDEAL (Persons raiding the hospital) SHOULD PREFERABLY BE GAN AIRM (without arms) BUT WITH STRONG ESCORT LEASMUCH (outside).

ALPHA. REQUEST YOU DO NOT INSIST THAT NA DAOINI BE GAN AIRM (people be without arms) AND LEAVE TO DISCRETION OF OIFIGEACH IC (officer in charge). BRAVO. ESCORT LEASMUCH (outside) PROMISED BY MAJ. HAUGHTON FROM QONR.

Col. Byrne said that his "ONLY REASON FOR GAN AIRM (without arms) SUGGESTION IS POSSIBLE REPERCUSSIONS IN SAN LIMINTEAR SIN (in that area) IF DONE LE AIRM (with arms).

Col. Bunworth replied that: "OP WILL UNDOUBTEDLY HAVE REPERCUSSIONS SAN LIMITEASTE SIN (in that area) AND PROBABLY FURTHER AFIELD", and that impressions would be determined by the local people "AS IT SUITS THEM AND THEIR REACTIONS WILL BE IN ACCORDANCE."

One very good reason why the members of the party should carry arms on the mission was that to get to the hospital from the airstrip, they would have to pass right through the middle of Manono.

Apart from the fact that "Operation Shamrock" would take place at first light, on December 2nd, no further information was given to Comdt. Beckett and the Nigerians, for security reasons.

The operation really began at 4.30 p.m. on December 1st, however, when the plane took off from Albertville. All ranks carried Gustafs and wore normal U.N. uniforms. An hour later, 30 minutes before darkness, the plane landed at Manono, ostensibly because of a shortage of fuel.

They were met by Comdt. Beckett, Maj. Edge, of the 4th Queens Own Nigerian Rifles, and an officer of the Moroccan contingent, and at a preliminary planning conference at the Nigerian headquarters, were brought up to date on the latest position. Barry's party now assumed responsibility for drawing up and executing the final plan of "Operation Shamrock", and in the discussions which followed, it was agreed that the Nigerians would provide additional troops for the operation, while the Moroccans would provide two trucks and secure the airstrip for the returning party.

Having retired to their allotted quarters, the Irish now worked out the finer details of the plan. On being advised by Comdt. Beckett that the Baluba retained their bows and arrows, spears and pangas, it was decided that members of the party would carry weapons but as they would be in a hospital, they would on entry have their weapons empty.

A problem arose, however, in that since the Niemba ambush the U.N night patrol had been unable to enter the hospital grounds because the main gate was padlocked and guarded by Baluba armed with "bundooki" and bows and arrows. After various solutions were considered, it was decided that the only peaceful method of entry lay in dressing up Capt. Condron as an accident case, and presenting him at the gate for "treatment".

Another problem was the possibility of fog preventing the plane from taking off in the morning. This was a very real possibility because of the low-lying area in which Manono was situated. However, there was nothing they could do about that, but hope for the best.

As the troops ate a rather Spartan meal of beans and soup they listened to Radio Brazzaville. By a strange twist of fate, the broadcast at that moment was a recording of the funeral in Dublin of the ambush victims, which had taken place on November 23rd. Having checked their vehicles for petrol and ease of starting, the members of the party retired for a short and somewhat uncomfortable sleep on chairs, couches and even on the floor.

Awake again at 4.a.m., they set out for the town at 4.45. Leading the way in Comdt. Beckett's old dark-blue Chevrolet car with its headlights on, were the doctor, the interpreter, and Condron, his arm in a sling, his head wrapped in a bandage taken from Quigley's leg and suitably stained with red ink. The remainder of the party followed in two trucks with lights switched off.

Through the sleeping town the strange little convoy drove, and arrived at a bend just short of their destination without incident. From there the three in the car went on ahead to the gate. Just as they approached, however, there was a movement high on their right. A woman standing in the light of a window on high ground on the far side of a wall had seen them and run off into the darkness.

The three officers paused and waited for the alarm to be raised. But everything remained quiet, and moving up to the gate they found to their surprise that it was both unguarded and unlocked.

A few minutes later, the convoy was driving away with seven Baluba warriors. "Operation Shamrock" had been carried out only just in time. Several members of the band which had slaughtered Lt. Kevin Gleeson and eight of his soldiers at Niemba, had already returned to the bush, and no trace of them could ever hope to be found.

There was a slight touch of dawn in the air as the vehicles drew away from the gate. But the orange and red blossoms of the beautiful gloriosa or climbing glory lily which Dr. Beckett had always admired so much in the trees outside the building were still shrouded in darkness.

Below them now, the troops could see the lights of the waking town. Suddenly a Congolese came cycling towards them. But he passed without suspecting that anything out of the ordinary was happening. The return journey through the town was accomplished without incident, and a short time later, the party was back aboard the plane.

After what seemed an interminable delay while the engines were heating, the plane took off in fine sunny weather and arrived back in Albertville at 7.10 a.m. There the Baluba were handed over to the Katangese authorities. The Irish had ensured that some justice would yet be done for the peacemakers of Niemba.

TWENTY-ONE

The Trial

In spite of the chaotic state of affairs in Katanga in 1961, the trial of five of the warriors went ahead. These were Michel Kabeke, Alexis Mukalayi, Stanislas Mwamba, Nufabule Banza, and Kamatshala Senga. The other two had been returned to Manono the day after their arrest as their story, that they had been wounded during a clash with gendarmerie in another area, was accepted. Presumably they had taken over the places vacated by two of the Niemba Baluba in readiness for their own departure.

Three charges were preferred against the five at a penal sitting of Elizabethville District Court. The first charge was that on November 8th, 1960, "on the main road between Albertville and Manono, and more precisely beside the Luweyeye River in the Niemba Region, Albertville Territory, they participated in a crime the object of which was to bring devastation, massacre or pillage . . ."

The second charge was that at the same time and place they killed nine U.N. soldiers, and this with premeditation, attempted to kill Kenny and Fitzpatrick, and inflicted three arrow wounds in Kenny.

Thirdly, they were charged that at the same time and place, they openly or secretly carried arms in an insurrectional movement.

When they appeared in court in June, they made a verbal request for the nomination of counsel to assist them in their defence, and the President of the Court made an order on June 23rd granting their request.

After several hearings in July and August, the case was adjourned until September 14th, but because of military events in Elizabethville at that time, the courts could not be held, and the case was put back until October 12th.

The military events referred to were the clashes which were then occurring between U.N. forces and Tshombé's gendarmerie in an inconclusive tussle to end secession during a period of chaos and confusion which saw the death of the U.N. Secretary-General, Mr Hammarskjold, in a plane crash. And here it is interesting to note that even though part of the U.N. forces which moved against the Katangan regime was Irish, the trial of the Baluba charged with killing the Irish troops continued, and is regarded here as having been a very fair one.

At the October hearing, the accused present stated that they had nothing more to declare in their defence, and the court closed the legal arguments and adjourned to consider its judgment.

The court delivered its judgment at a public hearing on Monday, November 13th, almost a year to the day on which Gleeson and his men had died in the ambush. Dealing with the charge of carrying arms in an insurrectional movement, the judgment, delivered by Judge A. de Bevere, stated that it followed from elements of the case that during the months of October and November, 1960, as part of an insurrectional movement launched in North Katanga, a group of armed warriors was set up by the customary Chieftain Kasanga-Niemba.

Statements were quoted showing that the aspirant fighters recruited by the chief underwent a ceremony of baptism in which they were sprinkled with "magic" water while the baptiser announced ritual words which were to shield them from gunfire. The recruits were then placed under the orders of the ex-Premier Sergeant Lualaba, who was entrusted with the job of conducting combat operations, the judgment stated. It followed from the terms of instruction given, that the raising of this irregular group had as its object from the start, to hinder and combat the exercise of order by the armed forces of the Katangese Government and to support in this way the insurrectional movement which had been started in North Katanga and among other places at Niemba.

On this subject, the judgment said, close relations were to be maintained by Chief Kasanga-Niemba with the leaders of this revolt. It was to hinder the movement of the forces maintaining order that the bridges were demolished and the barricades set up on the Niemba-Kiambi road after the Katanga gendarmerie had reoccupied the Niemba locality.

The destruction of the bridge over the Luweyeye and the construction of barricades were, said the judgment, the work of the people of Kasanga-Niemba. The judgment went on the say that the five accused acknowledged that on the order of Chief Kasanga-Niemba they received the war baptism, and were then incorporated into the group of warriors under Lualaba. They also acknowledged, it said, that on Nov. 8th, 1960, they were part of the group of warriors who, armed with clubs, bows and arrows and spears, lay in ambush near the barricades erected near the demolished bridge on the Luweyeye River. It was during that expedition, the judgment stated, that the armed attack on the Irish soldiers of the United Nations took place, and in doing that the five accused committed the crime of carrying arms in an insurrectional movement.

As to the materiality of the facts involved in the charge of having killed and attempted to kill the U.N. soldiers, the judgment referred to the "motorised column of the United Nations force billeted at Niemba" which patrolled the Niemba-Kiambi road on Nov. 7th. Here it appears that the Baluba alleged that on arriving at the bridge the soldiers were "refused" to be allowed through by Lualaba who, at the head of a group of Kasanga-Niemba warriors, "was guarding the barricades erected on the road on both sides of the demolished bridge," and that the patrol turned about "having warned the warriors that they would return the next day and would continue their route to Kiambi."

These allegations appear to have a rather hollow ring in view of the fact that according to members of the patrol the Baluba were guarding neither barricades nor the bridge when they arrived; that the Baluba who later appeared at the bridge were unarmed and apparently peaceful members of the local population; that the pretence was made that those in the bush were pygmies hunting; that a number of natives accepted food from the patrol; and that the patrol was under instructions to begin the return journey before a certain time.

The judgment went on to relate how on the morning of Nov. 8th, Lualaba led a group of about 100 armed warriors to the bridge, Chief Kasanga-Niemba having instructed them before their departure: "Either the Irish will turn back on the road, or else it is war, and you will win or die." This apparently emerged from statements by Kabeke and at a court hearing on July 7th.

The judgment described how, on arrival at the river, Lualaba had placed his men in ambush in the bush along the road and on both sides of the river. It told of the arrival of the patrol shortly before 4 p.m. and of the efforts of five of its members to find a place to take their vehicles across.

It related how, after about 12 minutes, the soldiers had rushed back, having seen warriors advancing towards them on the southern bank of the river, and how at that moment Lualaba, hidden in the bush on the northern bank had come out on the road and run towards the vehicles shouting the rallying cry: "Cartel".

Immediately, the judgment stated, he had been followed by his men who, screaming and brandishing their weapons, hurled themselves towards the vehicles, whereas the soldiers opened fire after the assailants had unleashed their first arrows.

Before the big number of assailants, it went on, the soldiers, of whom many had been wounded by the arrows at the start of the attack, had taken refuge in the bush so as to regroup on a small hill, where they were immediately encircled by the warriors who, under the cover of the high grass, had approached from all directions.

The judgment stated that it had not been possible to determine the exact part played by each of the five accused in the murderous acts and in the attempted murders committed.

All denied having personally given blows or wounds to the victims, said the judgment, and their statements on this subject seemed plausible. It was not unlikely that they might have been wounded and put out of action before having approached near enough to the soldiers to be able to make an attempt on their lives. Nevertheless, acceptance of that theory did not exonerate them from criminal participation in the crimes committed.

Whereas, the judgment continued, it was established that the five accused were part of the band which committed the crimes and were on the spot at the time these crimes took place, it must be admitted that they therefore took part in the actions in question, even if it was only by contributing by their presence and by their assistance in the culpable band, to the creation of the circumstances and the atmosphere which were necessary for the carrying out of the crimes.

It was of interest to note, the judgment stated, that the Irish soldiers did not open fire until the moment when the band of assailants was on the point of reaching them, and it might be deduced from this that the wounds proved that those who had incurred them, had left their hiding-place in the bush to take an active part in the murderous assault.

With regard to homicidal intent, the judgment stated that the five accused were obviously animated by homicidal intentions, at least from the moment when, Lualaba having given the signal to attack, they advanced in the group of warriors which went yelling towards the Irish soldiers. The fact that Chief Kasanga-Niemba had clearly evoked the possibility of a fight to the death at the start of the expedition, was enough to eliminate the last doubt on this point.

The judgment then went on to consider the question of premeditation. This, it stated, only existed as far as the carrying out of the crime might be separated from the firm resolution to kill by an interval which was sufficient to enable one to deduce from it that the author had reflected in cold blood on the import and illegality of his project. This interval only started from the time when the will was firmly and definitely determined on the act.

In this case, however, it seemed impossible to determine at what precise moment each of the accused decided to participate in the massacre of the Irish soldiers. It was plausible that it was only at the moment that Lualaba gave the signal to attack that the will to kill took the form of firm and definite resolution in the minds of the accused. It followed from this that premeditation was not established in the minds of any of the accused.

Dealing with the charge of participating in a crime the object of which was to bring devastation, massacre or pillage, the judgment stated that the relevant law required for its application that the perpetrators of the criminal offence would have aimed at one and the same time at devastation, massacre and pillage.

As it in no way appeared from the facts of the case that this complex aim was pursued by the accused, they would consequently have to be acquitted on that charge.

The judgment then considered the question of constraint, as all the accused maintained that they acted under constraint. It was necessary to examine, it said, if the constraint mentioned really existed and if it was of such a nature as to completely destroy freedom of action and so constitute a justifiable cause, or if this constraint simply meant a lessening of liberty.

In the first instance, it said, the accused pleaded physical constraint. They maintained that having taken refuge in the bush to escape the civil war, they were there apprehended by bands of young Baluba and taken to the village of Kasanga-Niemba to receive the warrior baptism and be enrolled in the armed group which, under Lualaba's command, perpetrated the massacre on the Irish patrol.

Although the accused had no direct proof of their allegations, the court did not ignore the fact that the recruitment of warriors in certain cases was accompanied by coercive measures. However, while at first the accused might have been under constraint, it was unlikely to have been exercised in such a rigorous manner and so closely that at no time was it possible to escape by flight or otherwise. Consequently, the constraint pleaded might not be considered as insurmountable.

Referring to the defence put forward, in the second place, of moral constraint, the judgment stated that it appeared that it was in obedience to the formal orders of their customary Chief Kasanga-Niemba that the accused made themselves culpable of the acts levelled against them. The very great authority of this Big Chief as well as the incontestable influence of the ex-Premier Sergeant Lualaba were such as to give the character of a tribal obligation to the orders given and to create a genuine fear of foregoing them.

The accused belonged precisely to that category of native which was still very much influenced by the customs of the rural *milieu*. By having suffered and followed the currents of collective psychology, they were ill prepared to take personal responsibility in face of events which could not fail to throw confusion into their minds. They had undoubtedly come under the influence of a demagogic propaganda which, under the guise of active nationalism, released suppressed ethnic and tribal complexes.

All these elements undoubtedly greatly deterred the free judgment and the freedom of action of those so frustrated. Nevertheless, the moral constraint did not constitute a justifiable cause unless it resulted from a very grave and imminent threat which gave the individual the alternative of submitting to the punishment or infringing the law, and left him no choice of action or of abstaining. The accused had been incapable of determining exactly what were the threats attached to a possible refusal to obey; they were not able to cite any such threats carried out on a recalcitrant subject.

Consequently, it could not be admitted that the threats which were weighing on them were "grave and imminent" to the point of completely annihilating their free judgment and so to constitute a justifiable cause.

Nevertheless, these factors very considerably lessened the amount of penal responsibility of the accused, and justified the decision of moderate penalties, especially with regard to Mukalayi, Banza, and Senga.

As the carrying of arms in an insurrectional movement formed the actual manner of participation in the killing of the U.N. soldiers, and so constituted one of the elements of this latter infringement, it followed that only a single penalty should be pronounced in the case of each of the accused.

The court therefore declared not established the charge relating to devastation, massacre and pillage, and acquitted the accused of it. However, it declared established in the case of the five the crime of murder and attempted murder without premeditation as well as the offence of carrying arms in an insurrectional movement.

The court, therefore, imposed the following sentences, after admitting extenuating circumstances:

Michel Kabeke—three years' penal servitude

Alexis Mukulayi—two years' penal servitude

Stanislas Mwamba—three years' penal servitude

Nufabule Banza—two years' penal servitude

Kamatshala Senga—two years' penal servitude

Tshombe shaking hands with Cmdt. Hogan. Col. Bunworth is in the centre.

Tshombe bows his head in prayer at the Mass at Albertville Airport before the bodies are flown home. In the centre is Col. Bunworth.

The troops render a salute as the last of the bodies are flown out of Niemba.

The last coffin is loaded on to a plane at Albertville Airport to be flown home.

Operation Shamrock successfully completed, the Baluba taken prisoner in Manono leave the plane at Albertville Airport. Dr. Beckett assists one of them.

The funerals in Dublin

RIGHT: Members of the 1st Infantry Group erect a cross at the site of the ambush.

BELOW: The cross erected, troops of the 1st Infantry Group kneel on the roadway as Fr. McCabe celebrates Mass.

TWENTY-TWO

Into the Lion's Den

Commandant Patrick Liddy, legal officer of the 37th Irish-U.N. Battalion in the Congo, shaded his eyes from the sun and looked up at the Palais de Justice in Elizabethville. It was a magnificent building, with steps leading up to its great Corinthian pillars, and he reflected that it was rather like the Four Courts in Dublin. Then he decided to have a look inside.

Chatting to one of the advocates about the trial of the Baluba convicted of the murder of the Irish troops at Niemba, he heard the strange story of how a police officer who had visited the area had learned from the local population of the place where Trooper Browne had made his last stand.

It was now almost two years since the ambush at Niemba, and all that time Browne had remained unaccounted for, although his gallantry had long become a legend. As Comdt. McMahon had reported, there was evidence that "one soldier was outstandingly brave. He was spoken of by the wounded in the hospital at Manono after the battle. The statements of the survivors would seem to indicate that this soldier was Tpr. Browne."

Browne subsequently became the first member of Ireland's Defence Forces to be awarded the Military Medal for Gallantry. The decision to make the posthumous award had been made on September 22nd 1961.

A statement issued on behalf of the Minister for Defence had stated: "A Board of officers was appointed by the Chief of Staff for the purpose of examining and reporting on acts of exceptional bravery or gallantry performed by members of the Irish contingent serving with the United Nations force in the Congo with a view to making recommendations for the award of the Military Medal for Gallantry.

"On the recommendation of the Board, the Minister for Defence has posthumously awarded the medal (second class bronze), to Trooper Anthony Browne, "A" Company, 33rd Infantry Battalion, and formerly of the 2nd Motor Squadron, Cavalry Corps, in recognition of his exceptional bravery when his patrol was ambushed at Niemba on November 8th, 1960.

"Trooper Browne endeavoured to create an opportunity to allow an injured comrade to escape by firing his Gustaf sub-machine gun, thereby drawing attention to his own position, which he must have been aware would endanger his life. He had a reasonable opportunity of escaping because he was not wounded, but he chose to remain with an injured comrade."

By November 8th, 1961, the first anniversary of the ambush, all had been done that could be done. The Browne family had received the Military Medal for Gallantry and, in common with the families of all the other victims, the United Nations service medal, while a plaque to commemorate our Congo dead had been unveiled by President de Valera in the Church of the Sacred Heart, Arbour Hill, Dublin.

Only one more thing cried out to be done—the return of Trooper Browne, still officially listed as "missing presumed dead."

A further search had been made for his body by the 1st Irish Infantry Group, under Lt. Col. J. C. O'Donovan, in October, 1961, after the group had been transferred from Kamina base to Nyunzu.

Niemba was then occupied by a company of Swedish soldiers. The Irish found the Niemba population—which was noticeably lacking in young men of military age—to be frightened though apparently friendly enough.

As it was near the first anniversary of the ambush, the group decided to erect a memorial at the scene, and an eight-foot concrete cross was moulded, a small crucifix presented by Fr. Phelim McCabe, the chaplain, being embedded in its surface.

The group had some difficulty in locating the exact site of the ambush, as local villagers were afraid to admit to any knowledge of it, and inhabitants of one village near the bridge actually gave the troops wrong directions.

Nevertheless, the rise on which Gleeson and his patrol had made their stand, was located, and on the roadside nearby the cross was erected. It was unveiled by Col. O'Donovan and blessed by Fr. McCabe, who also celebrated Mass on the road, using the back of a jeep as an altar.

There were about 60 members of the group at the ceremony, including also Comdt. Keogh, second-in-command, who had served with the

130

33rd Battalion. The local population was not represented, although the proceedings were undoubtedly observed from the cover of the bush.

As the inhabitants of the locality denied that there ever had been an ambush, no information could be obtained on the whereabouts of Trooper Browne, and searches of the area proved unsuccessful. There was, therefore, little likelihood that Browne would ever be found—until that day in 1962 when Comdt. Liddy paid a casual visit to the Palais de Justice in Elizabethville.

So it was that following correspondence between Lt. Col. Don O Broin, officer commanding the 37th Battalion, and the Director of Plans and Operations in Dublin—highly confidential so that no false hopes would be raised—Comdt. McMahon travelled on the plane taking the advance party of the 38th Battalion from Dublin to Elizabethville on October 24th. His colleagues knew that he was going on a special mission, but assumed that it was a legal matter.

The first thing McMahon did was to confirm the information which had been reported by Liddy, and satisfied from his own knowledge of the area that it was accurate, arrangements were made to recover the body. U.N. Headquarters was asked for permission to send a party to Niemba and to obtain clearance from the Central Government as the A.N.C., or Congolese National Army, was by this time in control of the Albertville area, including Niemba.

Meanwhile, it was decided that McMahon would be accompanied on the mission by Comdt. Sean Gallagher, 37th Battalion, Comdt. Heaney who was now with the 38th Battalion, and Capt. Jim Lavery, second-in-command of Browne's home unit, and now a section commander in the 38th Battalion's armoured car group.

These four held several conferences, at which they worked out details of their mission, in the 37th Battalion's operations room, formerly the office of the Farm Leopold, which was being used by the Irish as their headquarters. They discussed a red-pencilled map of Browne's reported location, and among other things, decided to take plenty of cigarettes which were always very useful currency when dealing with tribesmen, as well as some extra food for Fr. Peeters and his colleagues in the Catholic Mission in Albertville.

Eventually, clearance for the mission was received, and at 7 a.m. on Monday November 5th, they set out from Elizabethville in one of the U.N. planes ferrying oil supplies from Lake Tanganyika.

The first thing they did on arrival in Albertville was to work out the final arrangements with the Malayan-U.N. troops who were to provide them with an escort. Later that day they also visited the White Fathers, but did not inform them of their mission as the priests had enough worries of their own due to the recent chaos in the city.

Next morning, escorted by Capt. Ismail and three sections of a Royal Malayan battalion, together with an A.N.C. adjutant and four other ranks, and an interpreter, they set off by road for Niemba. As the A.N.C. were very pro-Balubakat, the difficulties and dangers of the mission could not be overestimated. However, the Irish officers were well armed. While Dr. Heaney carried only a smaller type .38 revolver in his pocket, for his own protection, the other three were each armed with a Gustaf sub-machine gun and 12 magazines of 36 rounds each, as well as a .38 Smith and Wesson revolver with 12 rounds of ammunition.

Niemba was reached at 2 p.m. There was some delay while the A.N.C. troops reported to one of their units now stationed in the "Guest House" as this garrison seemed to know nothing of the mission, and then the patrol pushed on down the Manono road, arriving at the bridge over the River Luweyeye at 4 p.m. The red-pencilled map showed Browne's position to be in the bush opposite the village of Tundulu which it indicated was on the left side of the road south of the bridge. Before proceeding to the village, however, the patrol paused at the cross which had been erected by the 1st Irish Infantry Group the previous year. Having read the inscription; "In memory of the Irish soldiers who died for the cause of world peace," the patrol moved on in search of the one who had never been found.

The village shown on the red-pencilled map as Tundulu, however, was deserted, and the members of the patrol found, just as Kevin Gleeson had found in villages two years before, that the local population had fled into the bush at their approach.

One old man who they did find, denied that that village was Tundulu and declared that there was no Tundulu. After visiting another village, which they also found to be deserted, they searched around without result, and then withdrew to the first village to consider the position. By this time they had come to the conclusion that the map was not quite accurate.

Then as they talked, an old Belgian army jeep arrived across the bridge from the Niemba direction, and a Congolese who was accompanied by several members of the A.N.C. garrison, presented himself as a local official and demanded in a highly excited manner why they had not reported to him on their arrival. His agitation increased when the discussion turned to the purpose of their visit, and while the offer of a cigarette helped to calm him down, he denied all knowledge of the body of any white soldier being in the area. He complained that all the local people had been frightened away and that they would not return until the patrol had left the area. The Irish, however, were adamant that they were not leaving without the soldier, and in the end the official agreed to try and contact the villagers. It was now late in the afternoon, and the patrol returned to Niemba to spend the night.

A fire was lit in the open, just outside the "Guest House" and the patrol prepared a meal. It was each nation to its own delight, and even though the food was rough and ready, it was very welcome. The Irish had stew, and never were Irish pack rations more appreciated.

The patrol took over the shop beside the trader's bungalow, and as Capt. Lavery noted in his diary: "We spent horrible night lying in old platoon house on the concrete floor. Nothing except groundsheets." The discomfort, however, was the least of their worries.

From what the interpreter told them, it was obvious that there was considerable unrest among the A.N.C. and the local population, as they could not comprehend why anyone would want to go to such lengths to recover a body, and feared that the Irish-led U.N. mission was a punitive one. The A.N.C. captain in Niemba had apparently told his men that this was a normal thing among white people, and that he had seen it happen before. Yet, should the frightened Baluba resort to aggressive action, it was felt that the A.N.C. would certainly side with them. The Malayan escort took special security precautions, and during a tense night all members of the patrol kept their weapons handy. But it passed without incident.

At 8.30 a.m. next day, the patrol set out with the local official and A.N.C. for the ambush area again, but now the Irish and their Malayan escort had made a decision which possibly saved their lives. This was that, among other things, the Congolese would not be allowed to slip away from the patrol to clear the way for another ambush.

This time, the patrol stopped about a mile and a half north of the bridge, while the local official had a lengthy discussion with a number of elders near a village in on the left which was now taken to be Tundulu. After some time, the Irish officers were invited to this meeting on condition that they came without the troops. The danger in doing so was all too apparent but there was no alternative if Browne was to be found.

Thus, having made up their minds that they would keep the Congolese in front of them at all times, McMahon, Gallagher, Lavery and the interpreter went in to the meeting. The elders were seated in a circle in a clearing, and beyond them in the bush the officers could see the huts of the village and a cluster of younger men. A chief presided at the meeting, but did not take much part in the discussions. His name, Comdt. McMahon later reported was Chief Kasanga-Niemba, the man who had organised the ambush of Lt. Gleeson's patrol.

It seemed that there was considerable disagreement between the elders and the local official. The elders appeared reluctant to admit that they knew anything about the matter, while the official seemed anxious to let the Irish have what they wanted and be on their way. The interpreter made a plea on behalf of the dead soldier, telling them that his "wife and children" were crying out for his body. Browne, of course, was unmarried, but this plea brought a murmur of approval from the meeting.

After about an hour of rather vehement exchanges between the official and the elders, it was agreed that the patrol would be shown where the heaviest fighting had taken place. The officers played along with this. Leaving part of the Malayan escort to guard the vehicles, the remainder of the patrol moved down the road with the villagers towards the bridge, and then it was suggested that they should search the thick bush on the right-hand side of the road. Making sure to mingle with the villagers, the patrol moved in through the bush. Then the official moved off at a rapid rate, doubling back up along the Luweyeye until he came to a spot north-west of the village and about mid-way between the road and the river. Lavery and the interpreter were close behind, and there, as Lavery later noted in his diary, "was little Browne".

At last, after two years, it was discovered what had happened to Browne. Somehow he had succeeded, though not without injury it would seem, in escaping the designs of the warriors who, during the ambush had rushed towards the sound of his Gustaf. Like Kenny, he too apparently thought of Albertville, or most likely the railway line running to it. Striking north, he succeeded in putting two full miles of bush and swamp between himself and the scene of the ambush. Like Kenny, he also, according to a villager, at some stage spoke to two people – native women – in the bush, asked them the direction of Albertville and gave them 200 francs to bring him food. However, unlike Kenny's experience, the women took the money and instead of bringing food, brought young warriors from the village of Tundulu. Wounded and exhausted, he could not possibly have hoped to win his second fight, and the patrol now found him where he had finally fallen.

But for the fact that the members of this patrol mingled with the villagers, they too might have been ambushed by the very same warriors. During the village conference and at the beginning of the search, the interpreter discovered 25 bowmen with four arrows each, lurking in the bush around them, ready to attack if they made a false move. Fortunately, a second ambush was averted.

Heavy rain was falling as the patrol left Niemba shortly after mid-day. During the mission, the Irish officers were to report, the adjutant of the A.N.C. "escort" had been against them all the time. Furthermore, it was learned that if, for some reason, they had stayed another night in Niemba, the Baluba, aided and abetted by the A.N.C., would have almost certainly carried out their attack.

So it was that Trooper Browne, who on Nov. 7th, 1960, had come to this forsaken place to join Lt. Gleeson and his men in helping a people who would not even help themselves, set off on Nov. 7th, 1962, to rejoin once more the peacemakers of Niemba.

• • •

Although the Niemba tragedy was a great shock to the Irish nation, it did not shirk its international responsibilities. It continued to supply troops to the United Nations Peace Force in the Congo. It is noteworthy that among the men who volunteered to carry out this essential international duty were a number of brothers of men who had given everything in Niemba.

When the operation came to an end in June 1964, many thousands of Irish soldiers had served under the flag of peace, and 26 had died in doing so. In a message officially thanking the Irish Government for the part its soldiers played in the operation, the U.N. Secretary-General, U Thant stated that during almost four long and troublesome years, the U.N force had worked tirelessly to fulfil its mandate. In that time much had been achieved and many of the dangers which threatened in 1960 had been removed. The military branch of the operation had performed its very difficult task with great courage and skill. The time had come for the force to be withdrawn, and its contingents, whose soldiers had shown so much courage, restraint, tact and gallantry, to return to their home countries. The U.N. and the world were in debt to them for the service they had rendered.

Of the 26 soldiers who had given their lives, U Thant said: "This high price was paid proudly in the service of the United Nations and of peace."

Author's Note

P.D. Hogan, who rose to the rank of brigadier general, always regretted the fact that his patrol, which was the last to search the area two days after the ambush, failed to find Trooper Browne. The report of the four officers who eventually recovered Browne's remains, didn't say how long they thought he might have survived. During my research in 1964, Hogan quoted one of the officers as saying that Browne lived for two days. However, Hogan is on record in *The Irish Army in the Congo* by David O'Donoghue, as saying before his death in 2004 that Browne was killed "some days" after the ambush. So, when did Browne die? Was he alive when Hogan's patrol withdrew from the area? Was he still alive the following day as Hogan suggested, when the U.N. flag was lowered and the Niemba post evacuated?

In considering these questions, I think it is important to set out the sequence of events in more detail. The ambush occurred on a Tuesday afternoon. On Wednesday morning the first patrol to arrive at the scene found Private Fitzpatrick, the first survivor, but had to withdraw because of hostile activity in the area. On Wednesday afternoon, two more patrols went to the area and recovered five bodies. On Thursday a larger patrol led by Hogan found the second survivor, Private Kenny.

Having consulted what Capt. Crowley called "an excellent sketch" prepared by Fitzpatrick, Hogan and his officers decided on the direction the search party would take. They found three bodies. Browne was not among them and even though the searchers had the assistance of Ethiopian trackers and a spotter plane, they could find no trace of him.

That was on the Thursday, and the following day, Col. Harry Byrne, commander of the Eastern Provinces of Kivu and Katanga, ordered the Niemba post to be evacuated.

The citation for the posthumous award of the Military Medal for Gallantry to Browne a year after the ambush, suggested that the officer board who recommended it believed he was killed at the scene when he drew the warriors away from Kenny. When his body was not found, there was speculation that it had been removed by the Baluba, whose custom it was said, was to take away the body of the bravest warrior after a battle.

However, as I recorded in my book, Browne did not die at the scene. Two years after the ambush his remains were recovered more than three kilometres away. A crucial sentence that was dropped from my story, presumably to make room for some last-minute corrections, recorded the actual distance: "Striking north, he succeeded in putting two full miles of bush and swamp between himself and the scene of the ambush." This sentence, which I have re-inserted in the new edition, was based on the report by the four officers of the recovery party. It read: "The bones were located about 500 yards from the river and some 400 yards from the road and approximately two miles from the scene of the ambush . . ."

A member of the recovery party, Captain Jim Lavery, told me they covered an even greater distance. He said that from the scene of the ambush they followed the river which looped back up towards Niemba. "It was very rough, bushy country with grass about three feet high. We continued along by the river . . . We covered about three miles . . ." (to the spot where the remains were found).

The report of the recovery party, dated Elizabethville, Nov.12th 1962, five days after Browne's remains were located, stated: "One of the villagers told the interpreter that the Irish soldier was lying wounded by arrows in the bush where we found the remains and that two women saw him and told the Jeunesse in the village of Tundulu who came and killed him." (The Jeunesse were young warriors and Tundulu was about a mile and a half on the Niemba side of the bridge.)

Lavery also said: "John (John Mokokha, the interpreter) told us later that everyone had run away from the village when the ambush took place, and had come back . . . Browne asked two women for the way to Albertville and gave them 200 francs for food. They brought young men from the village instead."

Kenny survived for two days and when found by Hogan's patrol was evacuated by helicopter from the village of Tundulu, the population of which had fled. "The village was thoroughly searched," Crowley recalled, "and though distant sounds of movement were heard twice, no African was found. The place seemed to have been deserted a few days previously. I should add that every village between Niemba and the ambush position was also deserted except for livestock."

Hogan said in his statement: "We continued our search covering a very big area of the bush very thoroughly but without success. We returned to Niemba reaching there in the late afternoon."

That was on the Thursday and Hogan's patrol was the last to search the area, leaving at 3 p.m. It's unlikely that the villagers would have returned while the troops were still around, so if as one member of the recovery party apparently suggested Browne was alive for two days, it does raise the possibility that the women came across Browne after the patrol left. Whether they came across him that afternoon, when there were still three or four hours of daylight left, or the following day when the Niemba post was evacuated, must remain a matter of conjecture.

Here I might point out that in spite of the very guarded, even hostile reception the recovery party received, Browne's remains may have been found because the Baluba wanted them to be found. Capt. Lavery told me they lay near the edge of a vegetable garden, a clear patch of ground about half an acre in size. According to the interpreter, when the people returned to the village the women went to the patch to get vegetables and that's when they came across Browne.

"The vegetable patch had not been used for two years," Lavery said. "You could hardly see the outline of it. The only thing that indicated the patch was there was the path leading down to it. They wanted the body moved so that they could use the patch. Their custom was to keep changing the patches and wanted this one back again."

This is in keeping with the information received by Comdt. Paddy Liddy, whose report sparked off the recovery operation. He told me that the police officer who supplied details of the location of the remains, said they were within a short distance of the village and time and again had been passed by villagers but not interfered with, probably because of superstition.

Over the years Kenny has been at pains to point out that Browne did not die saving his life, but it was not until 2006 that this was officially acknowledged. According to a report in *The Irish Times* on November

17th of that year, the then Minister for Defence, Willie O'Dea, apologised in the Dail to the two survivors for any trauma or grief caused by the fact that the record was incorrect. He said there were two principal areas of controversy—where exactly Browne died, and what Browne did to contribute to Kenny's survival.

On the first point he said a recent army report had concluded that on the balance of probabilities Browne managed to escape his pursuers, wounded or otherwise, making his way to the village of Tundulu only to be killed by hostile Balubas two days later. On the second point, he said the report clearly concluded that prior to his escape from the ambush site, "Trooper Browne fired his weapon at the Balubas who were intent on beating Pte. Kenny to death, thereby distracting them and saving his life."

In the course of two lengthy interviews which he gave to me in 1964, the notes of which I still have, Kenny told me he thought Browne drew the warriors off him while getting away himself. "During the fight he never said a word to me at any stage. I don't think he purposely saved my life, although he probably did in saving his own."

Browne's bravery, however, is not in dispute. Having fought off his attackers during the battle, he then managed to fight his way out of the circle of warriors and evade his pursuers. As Comdt. McMahon wrote: "There is evidence that one soldier was outstandingly brave. He was spoken of by the wounded in hospital at Manono after the battle. The statements of the survivors would seem to indicate that this soldier was Tpr. Browne."

A tribute was also paid to Kenny and Fitzpatrick in the Dail in 2006. The Minister referred to their horrific encounter with hostile forces, saying they displayed "courage, fortitude and tenacity in order to survive until finally rescued."

After reading *The Peacemakers of Niemba*, Maj. Gen. Dave Ashe, former Deputy Chief of Staff of the Defence Forces, said in a letter to me recently, "The bravery of those soldiers of all ranks, in the scenario they were in, was fantastic."

Tom McCaughren 2013

APPENDIX

The following is the text of the communiqué announcing the U.N. Defence Agreement:

Elizabethville,
17th October, 1960

COMMUNIQUE

General Rikhye, Special Military Adviser to the Secretary General of the United Nations, the ONUC representative and the commander of the Sub-Command of the U.N. at Elizabethville, held conversations with the President and representatives of the Katanga Government.

The disturbed situation in the regions of North Katanga was the subject of a broad exchange of views.

General Rikhye recalled the principles of the U.N. for the re-establishment of order by peaceful means, and proposed with a view to arriving at a rapid appeasement of the situation in certain regions, that the U.N. should intervene there in a more active fashion and it should carry out there defensive operations in a broader sense. He proposed, in particular, that all the important centres in these regions should be established as U.N. defensive localities, in which the presence of armed persons, other than the forces of order, would be prohibited. These localities would be demarcated in an obvious manner, in particular by signposts and notices prohibiting the circulation of armed persons. These localities would be defended with the degree of force necessary against the raids of armed bands and against attempts at looting. The same situation would apply to mining, industrial or commercial installations, and to points important for the economy of the country. In the remainder of these regions, the forces of the U.N. will endeavour to arrive at a complete pacification, in particular by intensifying patrols, by reassuring the population and by keeping the ways of communication open, and ensuring their security.

The occupation by U.N. forces will not exclude an effective collaboration with the Katanga Government and the existence in the occupied localities of the regular administrative and police services of that Government and the exercise of their normal functions. In these regions the Katangese Gendarmerie will continue to occupy its positions but will abstain from all active intervention during a period to be determined by common agreement between the Katanga Government and the Command of the U.N. forces.

Outside the regions agreed upon, the Katangese Gendarmerie will continue to ensure the defence of its positions by reacting only in case its positions or the ways of communication joining them are attacked by armed bands.

The following agreements were concluded by the Authorities of the U.N. and the Katangese authorities for the determination of the regions in which the U.N. would directly undertake the action described above:

1st Region—The territory of Nyunzu together with the post of Niemba, the Territory of Kabalo, the Territory of Manono, the Mulongo area in the N.E. of the Territory of Malemba-Nkulu, and the north of the Territory of Kabongo starting from Kitenge.

2nd Region—The region of Mukula Kulu, Luena, Bukama up to but not including Kabondo-Dianda

• • •

A directive (Directive No. 3) was issued the same day to all Unit Commanders in SCOMEP (Sub-Command Eastern Provinces) on the implementation of the agreement.

ACKNOWLEDGEMENTS

As I wrote in 1966, this book would not have been possible without the help and co-operation of many people, and I went on to list them as follows, giving the positions and ranks that many of them held at the time. First among those I would like to thank the Taoiseach, Mr. Lemass, the former Minister for Defence, Mr. Bartley, the United Nations Under-Secretary, Dr. Ralph J. Bunche, Mr. Ian Berendsen, also of the U.N. Secretariat, the Chief of Staff, Lt. Gen. Sean Mac Eoin, the assistant Chief of Staff, Col. Joseph Emphy, and the Director of Intelligence, Col. Michael Hefferon, and his staff, together with the staff of the Army Press Office.

My thanks are also due to the following Army and former Army personnel: Col. Harry Byrne, Athlone, O/C Western Command, Col. J.C. O'Donovan, Dublin, Lt. Col. R.W. Bunworth, Dublin, Lt. Col. P.D. Hogan, Dublin, Lt. Col. P.P. Barry, Cork, Lt. Col. Ferdy Lee, Dublin, Lt. Col. Art Cullen, Dublin, Comdt. Louis Hogan, Dublin, Comdt. E.J. Quigley, Curragh, Comdt. Sean Gallagher, Dundalk, Comdt. Patrick Keogh, Dublin, Comdt. Arthur Beckett, Cork, Comdt. Jim Breen, Dublin, Comdt. Fergus Fleming, Dublin, Comdt. P.J. Liddy, Dublin, Comdt. Patrick Jordan, Curragh, Comdt. M.F. Quinlan, Dublin, Comdt. Jarlath Gibbons, Dublin, Capt. D.F. Crowley, Dublin, Capt. Jim Flynn, Curragh, Capt. Jim Lavery, Dublin, Capt. Patrick Condron, Cork, Capt. Jeremiah Enright, Curragh, Capt. Brendan Deegan, Athlone, Capt.Richard Sloane, Athlone, Capt. Walter Raftery, Athlone, Capt. John Ryan, Dublin, Sgt. Jim Lynch, Dublin, Sgt. David McGrath, Dublin, Cpl. Patrick Anderson, Dublin, Cpl. Noel Hoyne, Kilkenny, Private Kevin Sullivan, Dublin, Mr. Patrick Ryan, Dublin, Mr. Peter Donnelly, Dublin, and Mr. Malachy Bartley, Surrey.

The reports prepared by the late Comdt. Malachy McMahon were invaluable, and I would like to thank also his widow, Mrs. McMahon of Athlone. I must also thank Fr. John Crowley, Cork, Fr. James Stone, Dublin, and Fr. J. Peeters, Albertville.

A special word of thanks is due to the two survivors, Thomas Kenny and Joseph Fitzpatrick, for discussing various aspects of the ambush with me.

Relatives of the men who fell at Niemba also have been of great assistance to me in the writing of this book, and my thanks are due in no small measure to Mrs. Imelda Gleeson, Dublin, Garda Sgt. Michael and Mrs. Gleeson, Goresbridge, Co. Kilkenny, Mrs. Elizabeth Gaynor, Leixlip, Mr. Charles Dougan, Dublin,

Mrs. Elizabeth Kelly, Dublin, Mr. and Mrs. Browne, Dublin, the Farrell family in Swords, Co. Dublin, Mr. and Mrs. Fennell, Dublin, Mr. and Mrs. McGuinn, Dublin, and last, but not least, Mrs. Catherine Davis, Dublin.

As well as making the information at their disposal available to me, many of the people mentioned above have been good enough to make available a large number of photographs from which the selection contained in this book has been chosen. In addition to relatives, the following supplied photographs: Col. Byrne, Col. Hogan, Dr. Beckett, Comdt. Gallagher, Capt. Lavery, Capt. Raftery, Capt. Sloane, Capt. Condron, Fr. Crowley, Sgt. Lynch, Sgt. Patrick Greensmith, Dublin, Mr. Donnelly and Mrs. McMahon, and for these I am deeply grateful.

My thanks are also due to Mr. Padraig O hAnnrachain, Director of the Government Information Bureau, *The Irish Times* and the staffs of several of its departments, particularly my colleagues Mr. Michael McInerney, that newspaper's political correspondent, and Mr. Dermot Mullane; Capt. Jack Millar, Aer Lingus, Dublin; and Mr. Joseph Noonan, cartographer, Dublin, for his maps.

I must also thank the Embassy of the Republic of the Congo in London for its co-operation.